FERMENT *Your* VEGETABLES

A FUN AND FLAVORFUL GUIDE TO MAKING YOUR OWN PICKLES, KIMCHI, KRAUT, AND MORE

Amanda Feifer

FAIR WINDS

© 2015 Quarto Publishing Group USA Inc.
Text © 2015 Amanda Feifer
Photography © 2015 Quarto Publishing Group USA Inc.

First published in the United States of America in 2014 by
Fair Winds Press, an imprint of
Quarto Publishing Group USA Inc.
100 Cummings Center
Suite 406-L
Beverly, Massachusetts 01915-6101
Telephone: (978) 282-9590
Fax: (978) 283-2742
www.QuartoKnows.com
Visit our blogs at www.QuartoKnows.com

19 18 17 16   3 4 5

ISBN: 978-1-59233-682-1

Digital edition published in 2015
eISBN: 978-1-62788-755-7

Library of Congress Cataloging-in-Publication Data

Feifer, Amanda.
  Ferment your vegetables : a fun and flavorful guide to making your own pickles, kimchi, kraut, and more / Amanda Feifer.
    pages cm
  Includes index.
  ISBN 978-1-59233-682-1
  1. Fermented foods. 2. Pickled foods. I. Title.
  TP371.44.F44 2015
  664'.024--dc23
                         2015024235

Cover and book design by Laura McFadden Design
Photography by Courtney Apple
Prop and food styling by Barbara Botting

Printed and bound in China

The information in this book is for educational purposes only. It is not intended to replace the advice of a physician or medical practitioner. Please see your health care provider before beginning any new health program.

To Jake, in gratitude for his fermenty and real life love and support. And for Ava, may she grow up in a world full of bubbly, probiotic acceptance.

Contents

Introduction | 8

Introduction

The act of vegetable fermentation is often as easy as chopping a vegetable, putting it in a jar, pouring in some salt brine, and waiting.

Yet for all its practical simplicity, fermentation is also amazingly meaningful and complex when considered from a political, social, or philosophical perspective. Fermentation is empowerment. The act of deciding to ferment one's food can be political. It says no to fast food and yes to the idea that good things come to those who wait. It says no to raging, baseless bacteria-phobia and yes to appreciating that we may not yet understand all that the microbial world has to offer. It accepts that innovation and exploration are important in a progressive society, but also that there are lessons to be learned from the past. It says no to ingredient lists that require a chemistry degree to understand and yes to foods with knockout flavors and simple ingredients.

Just salt and vegetables, when fermented, give us so much more than the sum of their parts. They give us sauerkraut, pickles, kimchi, and more. They give us higher vitamin output than there was input. They give us abundant probiotics and specialized enzymes that, researchers continue to find, do all sorts of unimaginably good things for our bodies, and even fight specific diseases. Undeniably, they give us flavors that taste like nothing else, flavors that can't be replicated by chemical additives or the addition of vinegar and spices.

This book is intended as a road map to fermenting your own vegetables at home. I hope that it calms any fears you might have about the safety of this extraordinarily safe process. I hope it shows you that, by being flexible and exploratory, you can experience both increased health and pleasure from your food. I hope, too, that it will inspire you to try not only these recipes but also to introduce your own favorite flavors into future batches of kraut and kimchi. I hope that it excites you and incites you to explore food through the world of ferments. Most of all, I hope that it shows you that fermentation is fun!

PART

1

Getting Started with Fermentation

The building blocks and basic techniques of practical vegetable fermentation are covered in this section, which is intended to be a reference point for the entire book. I'll lay out the basic aspects of fermenting vegetables, show you what you need, and address common concerns.

If you're new to vegetable fermentation, understanding the concepts outlined in this section will illuminate the step-by-step process of fermenting and give you an appreciation for what is actually happening in the jar or crock. This is the place to answer any nitty-gritty questions you have about process and to find out exactly why you should join the growing movement of home fermenters.

What Is Fermentation?

Vegetable fermentation is the transformation of a raw vegetable into something infinitely healthier and more delicious. Lactic acid fermentation, the primary fermentation process covered in this book, transforms vegetables into pickles without even a drop of added vinegar.

This transformation owes everything to the microbes in the soil and sugars naturally present in the vegetables. The soil is rich with bacteria. When vegetables are harvested, they come out of the ground covered in bacteria, including a small population of lactic acid bacteria (LAB, frequently referred to as probiotic bacteria) on their skins and peels. These bacteria, given the right conditions, will kickstart fermentation by feasting on a vegetable's natural sugars and converting them into a variety of things, including lactic acid, carbon dioxide (CO_2), and even a very small amount of alcohol.

The right conditions for lacto-fermentation are quite simple to provide: an environment with little or no oxygen and sufficient time at room temperature (roughly between 64 and 75°F [17.8 and 23.9°C] usually makes them happiest, although both lower and higher temperatures are sometimes used). Unlike some of their dangerous, pathogenic bacterial brethren, lactic acid bacteria do fine in the presence of salt, even in relatively high concentrations, so most vegetable fermentation also involves salting the vegetables.

Your job as a fermenter is simply to give those good microbes what they need and then get out of the way while they do their work. Once you understand the basic, practical principles, it's easy to see that fermentation is a process nature intended and one that you can nurture in a very hands-off way.

Why Ferment Vegetables?

Folks of all stripes choose to ferment vegetables for a wide variety of reasons. Some do it for the long list of unique health benefits, others for the taste. Some people want to eat more locally and some just get swept away by the feeling of power that comes from DIYing things that seem complicated (but are actually quite simple).

Flavor

One great reason to ferment vegetables is immediately evident with your first bite: the taste! Vegetable fermentation lives in a realm of food science that can seem like magic. Put some cabbage and salt in a vat and voilà! One month later, unseen microbes have transformed a humble head of cabbage into that tangy superstar sauerkraut. These flavors are difficult, if not impossible, to replicate without fermentation. That is one reason why great chefs all over the world are in love with this process. The words "tangy," "funky," and "perfectly sour" all describe the singular flavors that occur when vegetables are fermented.

Health

Fermented vegetables offer a surprising number of health benefits; the most discussed is their high probiotic bacteria content. There is new research published seemingly every day on the importance of our gut microbiome (our community of intestinal microbes). While the role that fermented, probiotic foods play in the microbiome is not yet fully understood, there is good evidence that probiotic foods play a role in the creation and maintenance of a diverse and healthy population of gut bacteria and that such diversity is important for our general health and well-being.

In contrast, scientific evidence continues to show us that a *depleted* microbiome, lacking in diversity, may be linked to many of the modern ailments found primarily in developed nations—obesity, food allergies, and even depression have all been shown to have either likely or established links to the health and diversity of our gut bacteria.

But probiotics aren't the only health benefits we get from eating fermented vegetables. These foods also have a higher vitamin content than their raw or cooked counterparts, meaning that when you eat raw cucumbers, for instance, you're actually eating a vegetable that is lower in vitamins than its fermented counterpart (see Classic Cukes, page 162). The fermentation process actually creates vitamins, and minerals become more digestible because of fermentation.

In addition, fermentation has also been shown to destroy or reduce certain compounds that are harmful to us, including pesticide residue.

This barely scratches the surface of the potential health claims currently being studied and the special properties that have already been identified. The area of health-related research on fermented foods is extremely exciting at present and will likely continue to expand in the coming years.

Preservation

A bunch of carrots left on the counter might get rather mushy and moldy after a week. In the fridge, they may last a couple weeks. If you ferment them, however, they'll become increasingly zesty and delicious; they'll turn into healthy, probiotic foods, and they'll keep for months or more, maintaining their crispness for much of that time.

The practice of vegetable fermentation can be traced back thousands of years. Long before there were refrigerators, freezers, airlocks, or airtight jars, people used microbes to secure their food supply for the colder months or to prevent spoilage in sweltering, tropical climes.

The fact that this practice has stood the test of so much time is one good indication that it's a safe and effective method for preserving food. If it didn't work properly, the fermenters of yore wouldn't have survived to pass their genes and their know-how down to us. For those of us who enjoy eating the produce of local farmers or maintaining a large garden, fermentation is a great way to keep those vegetables edible through the changing seasons.

Fun and Ease

Fermentation is for everyone. You don't need to be a sophisticated cook to make fermented vegetables, although the flavors that this process creates will have your friends and family thinking that you are. If you can chop a vegetable, you can ferment. Follow just a few basic and pretty flexible guidelines (outlined ahead), and you'll have endless fun fermenting vegetables to your heart—and gut's—content.

Ask a USDA Microbiologist

Dr. Fred Breidt, a United States Deptartment of Agriculture microbiologist whose work often focuses on bacterial competition in vegetable fermentation, has spent decades studying the microbes that make this process so safe and effective. He is an incredibly lively and knowledgeable source of information on the topic, and his enthusiasm is all the more inspiring because it is firmly rooted in research and hard science.

**On Whether Vegetable Fermentation
Is a Safe Process, Given Its Increased Popularity**

"Vegetable fermentation is one of the safest food technologies we have, provided, of course, that it is done properly. But it is really not that hard to properly ferment vegetables. The process is actually pretty foolproof."

On Why Vegetable Fermentation Is Such a Safe Process

Bacterial competition makes this process very safe. Lactic acid bacteria and the lactic acid they produce are extraordinarily effective at creating conditions in which their pathogenic competitors cannot live. Lactic acid is more effective than other types of acid (including acetic acid, the acid in vinegar) at destroying pathogenic bacteria, including *Salmonella* and *E. coli*. The ways that different acid molecules kill bacteria (in addition to the low pH killing effect) are currently being investigated. While *C. botulinum* spores do usually survive fermentation, they do not produce the botulism toxin when the pH is below 4.6. Since pH strips can be slightly inaccurate, the safest option is to only consume ferments that give a reading of 4.0 or below.

**On Whether Vegetables Are Safe to Consume After
Long Fermentation**

Lactic acid is an amazing preservative. Even in commercial production, some products are left to ferment at controlled (and often uncontrolled, in outdoor tanks) room temperature for a year or more. A pickle that has gone bad (which rarely happens) can be easily identified by off smells and appearance.

On Deciding When a Pickle Should Head to the Compost Pile

If there are aromas of extreme rotten egg or Swiss cheese, a fermented vegetable should not be consumed, although this probably goes without saying. When in doubt, use a pH strip. If the pH is above 4.0, don't eat that batch.

On Surface Mold

There are a variety of surface molds that may appear on the surface of a fermented vegetable. If you see a thin layer of yeast (commonly referred to as Kahm yeast), it's nothing to be concerned about. If a thicker layer of colorful mold has accrued, there is the unlikely possibility that this can start a very rare secondary fermentation that will actually raise the pH levels, making it possible for *C. botulinum* to sporulate in the bottom of the container. Again, a pH meter or strip can help you gauge the safety. At a pH below 4, the botulism toxin cannot survive.

The Safety Question

Okay, so at this point, you've read the word "bacteria" quite a few times. Freaked out? Don't be. Really. Not only are our mouths, guts, and skin teeming with healthful and harmless strains of bacteria, but the air we breathe and the soil beneath our feet are also havens for bacteria of all kinds.

There is no question that dangerous strains of bacteria exist, but on the whole, bacteria are not our enemies. The more we learn through scientific study, the more it becomes apparent that bacteria are an essential part of human life. Painting all bacteria with the same brush appears to have led us down the wrong path. If our bodies were sterile it would be difficult or, more likely, impossible for us to survive—one very good reason to set aside any remaining fear of bacteria.

The same things that help preserve fermented vegetables also make this process incredibly safe. In most cases, it only takes a few days of fermentation for the pH of lacto-fermented vegetables to drop to a level wherein it is impossible for the bacterium responsible for botulism, *C. botulinum*, to make its very dangerous spores. Nature provides the essential safety mechanisms here. You need only

Wild Fermentation vs. Cultured Fermentation

Although all lacto-fermented foods can accurately be referred to as "cultured", the term "culturing" usually refers to the practice of using a separate culture, rather than native yeasts or bacteria, to start fermentation. This could refer to ferments that require a starter to work (a kombucha SCOBY, or kefir grains, for instance), ferments that are cultured through contact with an already fermented substance (Misodoko, page 189; or Nukadoko, page 191), and sometimes even ferments that are kick-started with just a small dose of liquid from a finished ferment.

Wild fermentation refers to the process of fermenting foods with only the bacteria or yeast that are naturally present in the air or on the fruit or vegetable being fermented. With just a few exceptions, the ferments in this book are wild fermented.

While cultures are necessary for some types of fermentation, vegetables come equipped with everything they need for lacto-fermentation, and there is scientific evidence that using a starter can actually have a negative impact on the taste and texture of fermented vegetables, so going wild really is best.

chop, submerge, wait a few days, and accept that room temperature is just right for safe, fermented vegetables. See "Ask a USDA Microbiologist" for further details on safety.

The subject of this book is vegetable fermentation, so we're mostly talking about fermenting with lactic acid bacteria, but know that there is a wide fermentable world out there, in which other bacteria, yeasts, and fungi make many other remarkable fermented foods.

The Need-to-Know Basics

Ready to dive into fermenting your own vegetables? I promise you it's both simple and fun. With just a bit of planning and prep (probably less than you do for dinner each night), you'll be well on your way to making a batch of probiotic goodness that you can serve with nearly every meal.

The Main Components

Not much is needed to make pickles, kimchi or kraut. The vegetables themselves provide most of the essentials. If you're already chopping vegetables for a meal, you've already made it most of the way to a simple vegetable ferment.

VEGETABLES

The bacteria necessary for vegetable fermentation will primarily be on the peel or skin, so with the exception of onions and garlic, it is best to leave vegetables unpeeled. With inedible peels, such as those on some winter squash (Winter Squash Hummus, page 138), remove the peels after fermentation but before eating or just add some pieces of peel into the ferment and discard them after fermentation.

Wash vegetables for fermentation just as you would for cooking or eating raw. Avoid washing them in hot water or commercial vegetable wash, though, because either could have a negative impact on the bacterial life on your vegetables.

All vegetables are theoretically fermentable. In actuality, some don't taste great when fermented (although that is subjective), and others fall apart during

fermentation. As you kick off your fermentation habit, I recommend starting with vegetables with lower water content (think radishes and turnips over cucumbers and collards), but try them all to see what your favorites are!

Perfect specimens are not necessary for fermentation. While newer fermenters may have better luck sticking to the freshest vegetables, the somewhat shriveled, but still edible, roots you find in the back of the crisper can absolutely be given new life and saved from the landfill through fermentation.

WATER

The good news: a simple internet search will provide information on tap water in most municipalities. The less good news: some things that trickle through our pipes are not always super friendly to fermentation.

A chemical called chloramine is present in much of the municipal water supply in the United States. Chloramine, like chorine, is a disinfectant added to the water system to kill off pathogenic microbes. Due to its antimicrobial properties, it does have the potential to impact the success of ferments.

Unlike chlorine, chloramine can't be boiled out of water, nor will it evaporate if you let your water sit out overnight.

Brining vs. Salting

For the purposes of this book, *brining* refers to mixing salt and water to create a brine that is then poured over vegetables. *Salting* refers to applying salt directly to cut vegetables, so that they release the water stored in their cells. In both cases, the idea is to create enough liquid to cover the vegetables. The choice to brine or salt depends on the size of the vegetable pieces and the type of ferment.

Many of the recipes in this book were salted at 2 to 2.5 percent, or brined at 4 to 6 percent. There are exceptions to this, however, as some recipes lend themselves to a saltier or less salty brine. For example, the saltier brine used in whole pickled vegetables helps prevent mold and surface yeast and, of course, the no-salt-added chapter (page 177) relies on the salts naturally present in the ingredients to do what the added salt would normally do, as well as the acid created during fermentation to make them safe to consume.

To learn how to calculate salt percentage and for volume/weight comparisons, check out the salt charts on page 200.

Bottled water is regulated much less stringently than tap water and it can be next to impossible to get information on the origins of bottled water, or its contents, so save your money, and the earth, and use filtered tap water instead.

Despite the presence of chloramine in my local water supply, I've never had a failed ferment using even unfiltered tap water. If you have concerns about chloramine impacting your ferments, I recommend buying a standard charcoal filter (such as Brita or Pur) that will reduce or eliminate chloramine and other things (such as heavy metals) that you probably don't want in what you drink or ferment.

SALT

Salt plays an important role in vegetable fermentation. It strengthens the pectins in the vegetables, resulting in a crisper pickle. It gives an initial advantage to lactic acid bacteria over their salt-fearing, bacterial competitors, making ferments even safer. It aids in the preservation of fermented vegetables, allowing them to be stored for longer periods of time. It also provides some obvious flavor enhancements.

You can ferment with just about any salt under the sun, from cheap table salt to the often colorful, very expensive stuff.

As mentioned previously, fermentation makes minerals more absorbable, so using a higher quality salt, which is generally richer in minerals than table salt, can be a good choice for a little mineral boost. If it's in your budget, look for a salt with itemized mineral content. Many salts with a higher mineral content are very affordable, but if you prefer plain table salt (which works beautifully), look for one that has just one ingredient: salt.

Weighing vs. Measuring Salt

Weighing salt is undoubtedly the most accurate way to achieve consistent salinity, but that doesn't necessarily mean it's the best choice for everyone. In your home practice, I encourage you to find the salt level that best fits your taste. Consistency for you may mean always measuring with your favorite teaspoon and brand of salt, it may mean breaking out the kitchen scale, or it may mean salting to taste. So that you can achieve the exact results that I did if you so choose, the salt in all recipes in this book was weighed in both grams and measured with my favorite measuring spoons.

If you want to do it exactly as I did, use the gram weight, but know that measuring or salting to taste, rather than weighing, is completely fine for small batches. For crock fermentation, I do prefer to weigh, since small variations from one tablespoon (15 g) scoop to the next can add up to a big difference when using a large crock.

While salt levels do not decrease during fermentation, the increased acid in finished ferments does make them taste less salty than they tasted at the start. If you decide to salt to taste, you can achieve an ideal end product by making it slightly saltier than you like.

Too little salt will result in a quick-fermenting batch that is more likely to turn to mush. While the acid that is created during the fermentation process will make the product safe to consume, many people will find the mushy texture less than appealing. There are ways to work around that (see No-Salt-Added Ferments, pages 177 to 185), but using a 2 percent minimum for direct salting and 4 percent minimum for brining is the best way to ensure you end up with a crisp and tooth-some fermented vegetable.

Using too much salt may result in a very slow fermenting vegetable, a batch that fails to start fermenting, or an oddly discolored batch. Some strains of lactic acid bacteria will ferment normally at 8 percent direct salt—though a concen-tration that high would be utterly inedible without soaking and rinsing and is therefore not advisable.

If you're measuring salt, please check out the salt chart (page 200) for an idea of weight and volume differences between salts, but always let your palate be your guide.

Equipment

Vegetable fermentation does not require much special equipment; however, some normal kitchen tools are essential for making the recipes in this book.

- **Mason jars** make excellent fermenting vessels, and wide-mouth jars are much easier to pack than narrow-mouth jars. European-style jars (such as Fido and Le Parfait brand jars) with rubber gaskets and clamps are also very good options. When using narrow-mouth jars, the shoulders of the jar can be leveraged to keep vegetables packed and submerged under the brine.

- **Weight.** You will need something to use as a weight in your vessel, whether you're using a gasket-sealing jar or a mason jar. Many household items can serve this purpose. (See "The Tools of Submersion" on page 26 for options.)
- **Large bowls.** Having a larger bowl on hand is essential for direct salted ferments such as sauerkraut and kimchi. You'll want enough space in your bowl so that distributing salt evenly is easy and mixing and tossing salt into your vegetables doesn't result in a big mess on your countertops and floors.
- **Blender, food processor, or hand blender.** A blender of some sort will be necessary to make some of the recipes in the "Sauces, Salsas, and Condiments" chapter (page 27) and "Kimchi" chapter (page 101), while for many other recipes, it's just nice to have as a work-reducing device. Some people enjoy the process of hand shredding or grating cabbage for sauerkraut, but using the slicer blade of a large-capacity food processor can save you quite a bit of prep time.
- **Chef's knife.** A good knife greatly simplifies the work of chopping vegetables.

In addition to the above, here are some items that may not be necessary, but are certainly helpful:
- **Mandoline.** A mandoline is not necessary, but for those not gifted with great knife skills, it can make quick and easy work of creating uniform vegetable pieces.
- **Giant bowl or hotel pan.** If a large bowl is good, a giant bowl is better. I have very large capacity bowls that make it quite easy to salt, soak, and toss larger batches of kimchi and sauerkraut without making a mess. The wide diameter of these bowls also makes it easy to use a plate as a weight when I want to brine whole heads of cabbage for kimchi. Hotel pans, available at restaurant supply stores, work equally well.
- **Large liquid measuring cup.** Make easy work of mixing brine by pouring directly into a 4-cup (940 ml) liquid measure. You can also use a ½-gallon (1.9 L) jar for this purpose (measurements are marked on the sides), and if you have extra brine, you can always put the lid on and store it for your next batch.
- **Kitchen scale.** If you intend to weigh salt for the highest accuracy, a kitchen scale (with gram display) is necessary.

1 Cocktail Onion Rings (page 66), filled
   to 1½ inches (4 cm) below the rim

2 Foolproof Radish and Onion Pickles
   (page 44) with cloth secured as cover

3 Sweet Potato fry nests (page 65) with
   jar weight inside

- **Food mill.** For the smoothest sauces, a food mill is invaluable.
- **Plastic lids for mason jars.** These lids are pricier than the metal jar lids and rings that come standard with most mason jars, but they will not corrode if a bit of acidic kraut or kimchi gets stuck on the jar rim or in the threads. Plastic mason jar lids are not water tight, however, so don't go a-shakin' jars that are topped with these.
- **Fermenting crock.** For those looking to preserve an abundant harvest, a crock may be a good investment. For those who don't grow their own produce, a crock, although a tempting and beautiful item, is usually a more reasonable investment to make after a fermentation habit has been well established. This is the single most expensive piece of vegetable fermentation equipment you will be likely to buy, and for apartment and city dwellers, there are space considerations to take into account. See chapter 6 for more information on crock fermentation.
- **pH strips or a pH meter.** If you're planning on doing a lot of salt-free fermentation or making the only yeast-fermented recipe in this book (Garlic Honey, page 194), a pH meter or pH strips are advisable to ensure a safe pH.

The Keys to Successful Fermentation

There aren't many steps to successful vegetable fermentation. Most of the tips and tricks I provide throughout this book are practical details that I've picked up in my years of fermentation, and while they'll help you create your best ferment, most of them are totally flexible. The points that follow, however, are what you really need to know before getting started. Once you have these internalized, you'll know the basics of vegetable fermentation.

Key 1: Proper Submersion

A great way to protect vegetables from air exposure is to ensure that there is a thin layer of brine covering them during fermentation. Vegetable submersion prevents discoloration, as well as surface yeasts and molds from forming on the top layer of vegetables, and gives lactic acid bacteria their preferred, airless conditions. Submersion is a more important step for brined ferments ("Pickles," pages 39 to 69) than it is for packed ferments ("Kraut," pages 71 to 99) and for kimchi, where you can usually skip it altogether.

As you mature in your fermentation practice, you may develop a rhythm and a sense for how rigidly you need to approach the practice of submerging, but if you're just getting started, making sure that your vegetables stay beneath the brine should be one of your top considerations.

THE RULES OF SUBMERSION

To keep vegetables beneath the brine, you just need to apply a little bit of weight to the vegetables once they're packed into their jars or crocks. There are plenty of options when it comes to pickling weights, and if you prefer to keep your wallet in your pocket, creativity is key. You probably already have something in your home that could serve as a suitable weight for your fermenting vegetables. Here are a few guidelines that will help ensure best results.

- **Ditch the metal.** Unless it's restaurant-grade stainless steel, it's not a good idea to put metal in or on a ferment. Acids are produced during fermentation and metal corrodes when forced to sit on acid for days or weeks or months. Corroded metal is something you definitely don't want in or on your food.
- **Clean it.** Maybe this is a no-brainer, but whatever you're using as a weight should be thoroughly cleaned before sitting on top of your fermentation bio-chemistry. Soap (*not* antibacterial soap) and hot water will do the trick. A run through a hot dishwasher cycle also works.
- **Make sure it fits.** This may also seem obvious, but whatever object you use needs to fit comfortably through the *smallest* part of your fermenting vessel. Once things get active in your ferment, the CO_2 will push the vegetables up and may move the weight. If the weight is too large, it can crack your jar or crock, resulting in the loss of both the ferment and the vessel.
- **Open wide.** Using wide-mouth jars makes it easier to both pack your ferments in and to find weights that fit.

A variety of specialty and household items can be used to keep vegetables submerged during fermentation.

- **Search for safety.** Ingenuity drives fermentation experimentation, so I encourage you to consider any object in your house that might fit the above criteria and then consider whether or not it's food safe. Glass candleholders may seem ideal, but if they're covered in a glaze that isn't food or acid safe, that's definitely not something you want in your food. You can usually check with the manufacturer for details, but if you can't, seek another option.
- **Cover properly.** The specialty airlock fermentation systems (discussed further on the next page) are set once you close them, but for all other methods of weighting down your vegetables, you'll need to cover your jar in one of two ways. If the submersion weight you've chosen protrudes above the rim of your fermenting jar, use a kitchen towel, cloth napkin or large coffee filter to cover the entire thing and secure it by placing a rubber band over the cloth to prevent dust from getting into your setup. If your weight fits underneath the rim of the jar, cover the jar with its lid and ring, but do not fully tighten the ring. Leaving the jar ring somewhat loose allows CO_2 to escape, which will prevent your jar lid from becoming deformed during fermentation.

THE TOOLS OF SUBMERSION

Any number of items can be used to submerge your ferments properly. Many of the following are free or cheap or are household items you may already have.

- **A smaller jar.** This is my go-to method for submersion. Use a very clean, small jar (jelly jars, quarter-pint jars, or recycled condiment jars all work well). Fill the jar with water, tightly secure its lid, and then place it on top of the vegetables inside your larger fermentation jar. You should see the brine level rise over the top of the vegetables. Once this is done, you'll need to place a kitchen towel, large coffee filter, or cloth napkin over the jars and secure it with a rubber band around the threads of the larger, bottom jar.

  An advantage of this method is that it allows CO_2 created during fermentation to easily escape while the weight of the jar ensures that the brine level stays above the level of the fermenting vegetables. This liquid layer prevents excessive oxygen from reaching the vegetables, keeping mold and yeasts from forming. The disadvantage of this method is that it allows evaporation. This isn't an issue for a ferment of short duration, but for ferments of a month or longer, or in a very warm climate, you may need to push down on the weight or add more brine.

- **Glass or ceramic pot boiler disks.** You can buy these relatively cheap glass or ceramic disks at kitchen supply stores or online. They have good heft and can be stacked to create more weight if need be. Just make sure that the diameter of the weight fits through the narrowest part of your jar.

- **A boiled stone.** Find a round, flat stone that will fit in your jar. Boil it for 20 minutes and allow it to cool before first use to ensure that no unwanted microbial competitors survive. Avoid limestone and other sedimentary rocks that contain calcite, a substance that will react with acid and dissolve into your fermenting vegetables.

- **Ceramic pie weights or glass marbles.** These little spheres make great ballast when tied in a bit of cheesecloth or placed into a reusable cotton tea bag.

- **Vintage glass canning jar lids.** This suggestion came from a blog reader (phickle.com), Diane, who said she often finds these old glass lids at vintage stores for a steal.

- **Snack-sized, zip-top storage bags.** Put some of the salty brine into the bag (do not fill completely), seal the bag, and place it on top of the vegetables. Using brine in the bag ensures that if the bag breaks or leaks, the salt concentration of the ferment will not be altered.

If you'd rather purchase specialty equipment made for fermentation and submersion, there are several options you can look into.

- **Pickle weights.** You can purchase special fermentation weights that are specifically to fit in jars. They can be stacked to provide greater weight or used individually. Look for weights made by a reputable potter or company. Choose glass ceramic weights, with food-safe glazes.

- **Specialty fermentation systems.** As vegetable fermentation grows in popularity, new specialty products for keeping vegetables submerged while allowing CO_2 to escape are becoming more common. Current systems tend to be priced around $15 to $30 *per jar*, making them prohibitively expensive for those of us who have many jars going at any given time. If you're working on just one or two jars at a time, however, these might be a reasonable investment. These systems include containers or lids fitted with an airlock, such as the Pickl-It and The Perfect Pickler; detachable lids, such as the reCAP, that can be fitted to standard mason jars with a bung and airlock; and cap/compression systems like Kraut Source. Please keep in mind that despite some companies' claims, these do not make fermentation safer or easier. They *can* make it less odorous and neater looking.

Key 2: Proper Temperature

There are few things that impact a ferment more than temperature. Temperature influences the speed of fermentation and subsequently, its texture. The temperature at the start of fermentation even influences which strain or strains of lactic acid bacteria initiate fermentation.

This doesn't mean that fermentation is a finicky process, however. Between temperatures of 64 and 78°F (17.8 and 25.6°C), fermentation will initiate without a hitch (though some ferments taste better when fermented at a slightly cooler or warmer temperature). I find that sauerkraut has optimal flavor and texture when fermented below 70°F (21.1°C), as close to 65°F (18.3°C) as possible, while, for my palate, kimchi is the opposite. My favorite kimchis have been fermented at slightly warmer temperatures, between 70 and 72°F (21.1 and 22.2°C).

Some science disagrees with me on this—at least one study indicates that 68°F (20°C) is the optimal fermentation temperature for delicious 'chi, while others show a broad range, from 50 to 72°F (10 to 22.2°C), works best. This leads us back to a key principle of home fermentation: as long as you follow the basic, safe procedures laid out in this chapter, there is plenty of room for variation and preference. Often, we don't have perfect control over temperature, and that is totally fine. If a vegetable takes a very long time to ferment (too cool) or ends up too soft (too warm), then explore different microclimates in your home, such as near an air-conditioning vent, where it's cooler, or inside a turned-off oven or on top of a refrigerator, where it's warmer. And remember, the slight variations that happen from batch to batch are part of what make fermentation fun!

Key 3: Cleanliness, Not Sterility

If you've arrived at vegetable fermentation via canning or home brewing, you may be accustomed to a strict regimen of sterility. This is neither necessary nor desirable for vegetable fermentation. Microbes are our friends, and the particular bacteria responsible for vegetable fermentation are pretty good at taking care of themselves (and us), so step away from the sanitizer and vats of boiling jars and rely on elbow grease, plain soap, and water instead. Keeping a clean kitchen, clean jars, clean utensils, and clean hands is sufficient for safe and superior home-fermented vegetables.

What to Expect When You're Fermenting

Okay, so you're ready to let your ferments do their thing! How will you know that it's working? First, if you're using filtered water and fermenting at room temperature, it's *extremely* unlikely that fermentation won't initiate. Here are a few clues that will tell you things are going well.

How Ferments Should Look: Bubbles and Color Changes

You should see bubbles forming in your jar and/or foam on the surface when you're fermenting in glass. If you're fermenting in a water-sealed crock, you'll hear the occasional "bloop" that indicates things are bubbling along inside. Not all vegetables are very vigorous fermenters, and larger vegetable pieces will take longer to get active, so it may be a few days before you see anything bubbling. The bubbles in some ferments will be so active it may look like boiling water, while in others you see champagne-like bubbles along the jar sides or just the occasional bit of foam on the surface. When in doubt, you can use a pH strip. Below 4.0, you can start eating them if you like. Above 4.0, and they need a little more time to ferment.

The brine in your fermented pickles will also start to change from clear to cloudy in the early days, and you may notice a bit of white sediment forming at the bottom of the jar over time. Those are both good signs that fermentation is occurring. Vegetables with a brightly colored outer skin (red radishes and beets, for instance) may also shed their color, giving you very colorful brine.

When they're ready to eat, the fermented vegetables themselves may appear lighter (radishes) or darker (brussels sprouts) in color. The texture will have changed, but in most cases, it will be crispy, similar to pickled vegetables that you buy at the store. If you don't achieve quite the texture you want, try fermenting your next batch in a cooler spot or using a bit more salt in your next batch.

How Ferments Should Smell: Pungent and Strong

Ready for a little bit of straight talk? Sometimes ferments stink. For most people, this is a matter of getting accustomed to the smell or of being more selective with the type of vegetable used (just say no to open crocks of fermenting broccoli). If you're unfamiliar with the smell of fermented foods, try buying a container of living sauerkraut from the refrigerated section of the grocery store. Leave it at room temperature for a few hours until the chill is gone and then open it up and take a whiff. That smell—pungent, but not unappealing—should approximate what you've got brewing.

How Ferments Should Taste: Bright, Sour, and Salty

Fermented vegetables should taste sour and pickled. They should taste good, and most people love these flavors straightaway (although some *do* find them challenging at first), even if the aroma during fermentation doesn't always appeal.

A ferment that's gone bad will show signs: there will be colorful mold or the smell will be cheesy, musty, or moldy rather than bright and funky. The texture of the vegetables in an "off" ferment will be mushy. They will smell very unpleasant. If none of those things is true, give it a small taste. Bright, salty, sour notes should hit your tongue. If you've ever tried a deli pickle from a real kosher deli, you know how much more flavorful and complex those are than jarred, supermarket pickles. Those are a few of the flavors you should expect, but these foods are complex, so other flavors aren't uncommon. The unpleasant notes describe above are not common occurrences, and they are easily avoided by using the simple techniques laid out in this section.

Troubleshooting and FAQs

Following are some of the most common issues and questions I have received when teaching fermentation. Refer back to this section as needed—or just to soothe your fears before beginning.

"When is it done?"

It's done when you like the flavor and acidity, and that's when it should be moved to the fridge. While the recipes in this book all mention specific time frames, you should feel free to ferment them longer if you feel that they are not yet sour enough. The warmer the jar, the faster it will ferment.

Fermented foods are dynamic and alive. Even putting them into the refrigerator won't completely stop the fermentation process in most cases. Expect to taste something slightly different each time you open your jar. The longer it ferments, the more sour it will get.

"My brine is cloudy and there's white sediment at the bottom."

White sediment is the normal accumulation of bacteria and yeast in a ferment. Some vegetables (hot peppers, page 133, and snap peas, page 49) tend to accumulate more sediment than others, but it is nothing to be concerned about.

Cloudy brine in pickles is also normal. It isn't related to the type of salt you use—it is related to the fermentation process itself.

"What do I do with a batch that has gone moldy?"

The presence of mold or visible yeast on the surface of a fermented vegetable may indicate that there was some air exposure, which is not in itself worrisome. However, if there is an abundance of dark- or bright-colored mold, that batch should be tossed. If there is a whitish mold or yeast on the surface, you have some options. The most important thing to do is skim the mold immediately to keep it from forming a thicker layer and then test the ferment with a pH strip. If the pH is below 4.0, it is safe to consume. For salted ferments, I generally use the sniff test: if it smells like a tasty, sour ferment, eat it. Small amounts of beige or white mold are harmless, but a pH strip will always tell you if an undesirable secondary fermentation has made your ferment unsafe. This has never happened to me, and even in the scientific literature it is extremely rare.

"My ferment is mushy."

A mushy ferment usually indicates too little salt, a fermenting temperature that was too high, a too-long fermentation period, or the use of a starter. If your ferment still smells good and sour, it is still okay to eat. If the texture is unpleasant to you, consider puréeing it into a sauce, dip, dressing, soup, or stew.

To avoid this problem next time, try moving your ferment to a slightly cooler spot in your home and raising the salt content a bit. And definitely skip the starter if you used one! It's not necessary.

"My sauerkraut is pink and I used green cabbage."

Green kraut turned pink indicates that you used too much salt or that the salt wasn't properly distributed at the start of fermentation. Eating kraut discolored in this way isn't recommended.

"Is there anything I can do to reduce the … aroma?"

If you find the smell very bothersome, there are a few things you can do. First, be aware that some vegetables have a stronger fermenting smell than others. Kimchi with fish sauce, cauliflower, brussels sprouts, and broccoli can definitely clear a room. Fermenting stinkier vegetables in an airlock system or water-sealed crock can reduce or eliminate the odors. Some people also have a corner of the pantry or a special closet or cupboard dedicated to fermenting vegetables.

One tip for anyone sensitive to these smells: chill ferments in the fridge before opening to eat. It's a great way to tame odors and stoke appetites.

"My batch is a little slimy."

Did you use a starter? If so, don't do that again.

If not, it is likely a case of too-sweet vegetables like beets or carrots that favored yeast fermentation (undesirable in this case) over lactic acid fermentation (desirable).

While you can cut most vegetables into any size and shape you'd like, for sweeter roots, use larger pieces to keep those sugars from becoming too available.

"There are bubbles in my jar!"

Bubbles are a good thing and proof that fermentation is happening. The production of CO_2 is a natural and normal part of vegetable fermentation.

"There are no bubbles in my fermentation vessel."

Are you 100 percent sure that there are absolutely no bubbles? Not every vegetable ferments super vigorously, so with certain vegetables at cooler temperatures, sometimes you'll just see some light bubbling in the early days. If you definitely never saw any bubbling, that may indicate that fermentation never initiated. Possible culprits are an overly chilly environment, disinfectants in the water supply, or irradiated produce. Smell for fermenty aromas and keep a close lookout for surface bubbles.

Give it some more time and if there is still no sign of life, consider the above culprits and start anew.

"It stopped bubbling! Did I kill my ferment?"

Unless you cooked it, it's very unlikely that the bacteria in your ferment just up and died. Vegetable ferments are more actively bubbly during the early days of fermentation in most cases (there are notable exceptions to this, so don't worry if it continues to bubble, either). The bacteria that are active at the start of fermentation generally produce more CO_2 than the bacteria that are active later in the process, so it's more than likely that things just quieted down.

"What's the ideal temperature for vegetable fermentation?"

There is an ideal range of 64 to 75°F (17.8 to 24°C), but this is flexible. The exact ideal temperature varies from one ferment to another, by one bacterial strain to another, and by taste preference. In my own practice, I have found that a broad range of room temperatures, some of them beyond the boundaries of this range, will end in a tasty ferment.

"I keep my home cooler/warmer than this. Can I still ferment?"

Yes. Take a little survey of your home. You will probably find that there are warmer or cooler microclimates in spots near an air-conditioning or heating vent, in a cold closet or basement, on top of a refrigerator, or inside a (turned-off) oven. If you truly can't find a spot within this range, give it a shot anyway. If your temperatures are warmer, add a bit more salt, cut fermentation times, and check regularly for mushiness. If your temperatures are too cool but still above 50°F (10°C), allow for a much longer fermentation period.

"Are these foods safe to eat after sitting at room temperature for so long?"

Yes. Fermenting foods at room temperature makes them safer to eat than raw or cooked vegetables. The lactic acid created during fermentation makes it impossible for bad bacteria to blossom. This process works best somewhere between 64 and 75°F (17.8 and 24°C).

"Will I get botulism/die from eating these foods?"

No. Although humans have been fermenting for thousands of years, there are *zero* reported cases of botulism associated with eating fermented vegetables. The same cannot be said for any other preservation process or even of raw vegetables. This process is extremely safe.

"Are fermented vegetables raw food?"

Yes. Heating vegetables above 110°F (43.3°C) or so will kill many of the bacteria responsible for successful vegetable fermentation.

"Is it okay to cook with ferments?"

Cooking ferments will kill the probiotic bacteria, but the flavors that fermented foods contribute to finished dishes usually make it well worth the occasional bacterial sacrifice. Keeping fermented vegetables below approximately 110°F (43.3°C) is best for keeping the probiotic bacteria alive and kicking.

"Is there really alcohol in these?"

Yes, there is a small amount of alcohol in fermented vegetables. In the U.S., any food or drink containing less than 0.5 percent (1 percent in many other countries) alcohol need not be labeled as containing alcohol, so while there is a tiny amount, it's not enough to even warrant a label. You may be surprised to find that many items on the grocery store shelf that you already eat contain small amounts of alcohol. In fermented vegetables, we're talking about trace amounts and certainly nothing that is unsafe to feed to a child or teetotaler. Garlic Honey (page 194), the only yeast ferment in this book, has the potential to develop an alcohol content similar to that of a lower-alcohol mead.

"Is there anything I should consider when purchasing produce?"

Some imported produce is irradiated and will therefore not ferment. Irradiated produce is required to be labeled in the U.S. and Canada, but you may need to read the label very carefully to find the relevant text. Pay particular attention to fresh ginger and hot peppers, as these are frequently imported and irradiated. One more great reason to buy local and organic!

"How do I know whether the sauerkraut/pickles/kimchi I buy at the store is/are probiotic?"

Canned vegetables sitting on the shelf in the store do not contain living, probiotic bacteria. Look for probiotic versions in the refrigerated aisle, with labels that say "contains live, active cultures" or something similar. These are probiotic.

You can also look online for small, local fermentation companies in your area. Transporting fermented foods can be tricky and expensive for producers, so the highest quality products will probably be made by a local company. Wonderfully, there are more local producers popping up all the time!

"Is there any vegetable I can't ferment?"

Theoretically, no. Everything that grows in the earth has a native population of lactic acid bacteria that will undertake the work of fermentation in the right conditions. Some vegetables are more likely to result in a delicious and crispy end product due to their texture and water content, however.

Kale tends to get bitter and leafy greens like spinach and chard tend to mush quickly and produce less than desirable flavors, but don't limit yourself! Anything you have in abundance is worth trying. Start small with new-to-you vegetables.

On to the Recipes!

Sometimes, when you're getting started, you just want someone to tell you exactly what to do. For that reason, detailed instructions are laid out in recipes throughout this book. Be aware that there are many different ways to approach this process, and if you've found a way that works for you, keep on keepin' on! Happy fermenting!

PART

2

Small-Batch Lactic Acid Fermentation

Now that you've got the basics, you're ready to get started. In this part, we'll cover all sorts of recipes for pickles, kraut, kimchi, and more.

Most of these recipes call for batches of one quart or less. This way, you're not stuck with 3 gallons (11.4 L) of pickles you don't love, and you're free to experiment with as many ferments as you like. You can choose whatever submersion method suits your home and your resources. This section is all about fun, flexibility, and letting time and microbes make things delicious.

CHAPTER ONE

Pickles

When most people picture a pickle, they think of a big juicy, sour dill cucumber from the kosher deli. Those are, admittedly, pickles worthy of their iconic status, but the world of pickles is so much more than cucumbers. Pickles can be anything, from sliced beets (Cumin Basil Beets, page 46) to jicama sticks (Pickle My Jicama, page 49) to julienned rutabaga (Rosemary Rutabaga, page 60).

Pickles are one of the easiest ferments to make. They require few ingredients and ferment for a relatively short time before they're ready to be enjoyed.

Although kimchi and kraut are also pickled vegetables and, technically speaking, this entire book is a book of pickles, for the purposes of this chapter, a pickle will be a vegetable that is fermented, whole or chopped, in saltwater brine, or, if directly salted, a vegetable that isn't cabbage.

Let's Pickle That!

Getting started is very easy. You only need three ingredients—vegetables, salt, and water—and some kind of container (large jars work well; see pages 20 to 23 for more options). Just about any vegetable, from kohlrabi to carrots, can be fermented into flavorful, healthful, delicious pickles. Some vegetables have more universal appeal and effortlessly ferment into crispy, flavor-rich pickles (see Foolproof Radish and Onion Pickles, page 44), while others require a bit more attention (Classic Dill Pickle Spears, page 68).

The Rules, If You Can Call Them That

There are honestly not that many rules to pickle fermentation. You mostly want to rely on the things that give you a result that tastes good to *you*. However, there are a few things that are usually necessary for safety and excellent results.

CHOP YOUR VEGETABLES

Chopping vegetables exposes more surface area, making the vegetable's natural sugars more available to the lactic acid bacteria. Bacteria need access to their "food" to efficiently do the work of fermentation.

SUBMERGE AND COVER

If you fear mold, or surface yeast, or a less than tasty batch, proper submersion is your friend. Ensure that your pickles stay submerged under a thin layer of brine during the fermentation period. There are several methods for doing this, as detailed in part one (pages 23 to 28).

GIVE IT TIME

For most vegetables, anything less than three days of fermentation time is likely to be insufficient for the pickle to reach a pH of 4.6, the level of acidity at which it is impossible for *C. botulinum* to survive. If you want to be extra certain that your pH is low enough, you can purchase pH strips online, at any homebrew store, and even at many drugstores, but the truth is, that's generally not necessary. At three days, most ferments won't taste nearly acidic enough to eat. At four to five days of room temperature fermentation there is little chance that a fermented vegetable is above a pH of 4.6. For most pickle lovers, that would be the earliest that the flavor would be developed enough to bother eating them.

The jar on the left looks good. The jar on the right will be more prone to surface yeasts.

FIND THE RIGHT FIT

Submersion is essential, but don't fill your jar halfway with veggies and then fill the jar with brine. Jars that aren't mostly full of vegetables are more likely to develop surface molds or yeasts.

Conversely, too little space in a cramped jar with vegetables that don't stay submerged can also be an invitation to surface mold. An overly cramped jar might also overflow once the CO_2 starts bubbling, leaving you with messy counters and a jar that needs topping off.

My best rule of thumb for jar fermentation is to add vegetables until your jar is full to about 2 inches (5 cm) below the jar rim and to then submerge them under a ¼ to a ½ inch (5 mm to 1.5 cm) of brine, leaving 1½ inches (4 cm) of space at the top of the jar before the weight is added. When starting out, it's a great practice to place your jars on plates or bowls, just in case there is any overflow.

LOSE YOUR COOL

I know. Your mom told you to toss food out if it accidentally sat on the counter overnight. No disrespect to your mother, but unlike other foods, ferments are actually safer when left at room temperature. My ideal fermentation temperature for pickles is between 68 and 72°F (20 and 22.2°C) and a temperature between 64 and 78°F (17.8 and 25.6°C) is most likely to provide your bacteria with the right conditions to do the work of acidifying your food. Refrigerator temperatures will sometimes keep fermentation from starting and will always slow it down dramatically, so don't put ferments in the fridge until *after* they've been fermented to your liking.

TRY NEW THINGS

Vegetable fermentation requires very little rule following. That said, all of the recipes in this book have been carefully tested, and I do recommend that you follow them exactly if you want the same results I had. In the future, feel free to use this book as a jumping-off point in your fermentation experimentation. Salt levels, vegetable combinations, timing, and seasonings are, with few exceptions, adaptable to your preferences. As long as you follow the guidelines detailed in part one, it's safe to experiment with these recipes. See a seasoning you don't like? Leave it out. Have a brainstorm for an addition you think would work? Go for it. Let creativity, seasonality, and taste be your guides.

Not All Pickles Are Created Equal: Canned Pickles vs. Fermented Pickles

Canning is a preservation method through which vegetables are acidified with hot vinegar. The vinegar adds acidity and, along with other seasonings, gives canned pickles their flavor. Canned pickles are then given a long, boiling hot water bath to kill off all microbial activity (most specifically the bacterium responsible for botulism—which is very heat tolerant—but also all of the good-for-us, probiotic, lactic acid bacteria). This process allows for sealed jars to be stored at room temperature for long periods of time, often a year or more. The pickles you find on grocery store shelves are produced using this method.

Canned pickles are not living foods. They are shelf stable, so they will taste virtually the same when you take them out of the jar as they did the day they were put in. Like all cooked foods, they generally have fewer vitamins than the raw vegetables from which they're made, they are not probiotic, and they have no special health benefits.

Fermented pickles are the opposite of canned pickles. Rather than sterilization, fermentation relies on the cultivation of good bacteria, which unfailingly do the work of keeping the bad guys at bay. These lactic acid bacteria, naturally present on all vegetables, eat the vegetable sugars and convert them into lactic acid and CO_2 (see all those bubbles?), among other things. This process quickly and naturally eliminates the dangers posed by bad bacteria and results in a probiotic, good-bacteria-filled pickle.

Fermented pickles should usually be stored at cooler temperatures once you're happy with their flavor, but, because they are living foods, their flavor and texture will continue to change over time, even in the refrigerator. Depending on your taste preferences, the vegetable used, salt levels, and how your pickles are made and stored, they may keep for a week or for more than a year.

Unlike their canned cousins, fermented vegetables boast many notable health benefits, from loads of healthy probiotics to increased vitamin content and improved nutrient absorption.

Ingredients

½ pound (225 g) large heirloom or cherry belle radishes, trimmed and unpeeled

½ small onion (2 ounces, or 50 g), peeled and sliced into thin rounds

1½ teaspoons (9 g) kosher salt

1 cup (235 ml) filtered water

FOOLPROOF RADISH AND ONION PICKLES

Start here. In a pretty foolproof process, radish pickles remain an especially easy first step. I always have a jar of plain radish pickles fermenting at my house, simply because they're so easy to make and taste so good that we tend to eat the whole jar very quickly. These make a great base for gluten-free, low-carb, paleo, and vegan appetizers, but to be honest, I usually just eat them French style, topped with a bit of cultured butter or entirely without adornment.

Cut any soft or visually unappealing parts out of the radishes, but leave as much as possible intact. Slice into ¼-inch (0.5 cm) thick rounds. Layer radish and onion slices into a wide-mouth pint (500 ml) jar. There should be about 1½ inches (4 cm) of space between the radishes and the rim of the jar once they're all in.

Mix the salt into water until dissolved and pour this brine over the radishes, ensuring that there is a thin layer of brine over the vegetables. You may need to push the radishes down with a clean finger to gauge the fullness of the jar.

Using your preferred method (see pages 23 to 28), submerge your veggies and cover your jar.

Place your jar on a small plate or bowl and allow to ferment at room temperature for 6 days to 2 weeks.

Once your happy with the flavor and acidity, remove the weight, secure the lid, and place the jar in the fridge. Enjoy chilled.

Yield: 1 pint (450 g)

Ingredients

- 4 or 5 medium-small beets (1 pound or 450 g), any variety, trimmed but unpeeled
- 1½ teaspoons (3.5 g) cumin seeds
- 1 tablespoon (18 g) kosher salt
- 2 cups (470 ml) filtered water
- ⅛ cup (3 g) whole basil leaves, tightly packed or one 6-inch (15 cm) stem basil, for use post-fermentation

CUMIN BASIL BEETS

The flavors in this recipe were matched out of necessity. I had a garden full of basil and a spice rack that was empty, save a container of cumin seeds. It was serendipity, because I don't think I would have discovered this favorite combo if I'd had other options. To date, this remains one of the most popular pickle recipes on my blog, and each year at the start of beet season, I get at least a few kind emails telling me that they are the "best pickles ever."

Slice the beets into ¼-inch (0.5 cm) slices.

Put the cumin seeds in the bottom of a quart jar (1 L) and stack the beet slices on top.

Mix the salt into water until dissolved and pour the brine into the jar until the beets are just covered.

Using your preferred method (see pages 23 to 28), submerge your veggies and cover your jar.

Place the jar on a small plate or bowl and allow to ferment at room temperature for 1 to 2 weeks.

Once you're happy with the flavor and acidity of the beets, remove the weight, pack the basil leaves into the jar, put the lid on, and stick them in the fridge.

After 2 days, remove the basil. Enjoy the pickles at any time. Store in the fridge.

Yield: 1 quart (900 g)

Using Herbs and Spices

Herbs: Woody herbs like thyme and rosemary hold up just fine in brine, but leafier herbs like fresh basil, mint, and oregano may do better if added just at the end of fermentation and removed after a couple of days of infusing. Try it both ways. The worst thing that can happen is that the herbs will break down a bit and the flavor of the herbs may not be as pronounced as you might like.

Spices: I prefer whole spices and seeds whenever possible in a brined ferment. Powdered spices are sometimes difficult to keep submerged, and anything floating on the surface can invite unappealing surface yeasts. This isn't a 100 percent rule, but it's something to keep in mind when you have the option or if you do end up with unexplained surface yeasts.

Ingredients

- ½ medium, unwaxed rutabaga (½ pound, 225 g)
- 1 inch (2.5 cm) of trimmed, unpeeled ginger
- 1 tablespoon (15 g) grated, unpeeled horseradish root
- 1½ teaspoons (9 g) kosher salt
- 1 cup (235 ml) filtered water

RUTABAGA HORSERADISH GINGER PICKLES

I am a latecomer to the pleasures of fresh horseradish. Aside from a certain sauce from a certain fast food restaurant that I *adored* as a kid, I pretty much ignored this knobby root until just a few years ago. When I started buying the fresh root and grating it, I loved what small quantities added. In this recipe, its flavor balances the natural sweetness of the rutabaga, while the fermentation process itself tames the horseradish. These pickles would make a great addition to a roast beef sandwich.

Trim the top off of the rutabaga. Remove and discard any unattractive, soft, or rooty bits, but leave it otherwise unpeeled.

Cut the rutabaga into ½-inch (1.5 cm) thick, 3- to 4-inch (7.5 to 10 cm) long batons. Slice the ginger into thin rounds, cutting out any soft parts or tough-to-clean crevices.

Place the horseradish and ginger in the bottom of a pint (500 ml) jar and stand the rutabaga sticks on top of them, tilting the jar to the side a bit to make room to slide the pieces in more easily.

Mix the salt into water until dissolved and pour the brine into the jar, ensuring that there is a thin layer of brine over the top of the rutabaga.

Using your preferred method (see pages 23 to 28), submerge your veggies and cover your jar.

Place your jar on a small plate and allow to ferment at room temperature for 10 days to 3 weeks.

Once you're happy with the flavor and acidity, remove the weight, secure the lid, and place the jar in the fridge.

Yield: 1 pint (450 g)

Ingredients

¼ pound (115 g) any combination of zucchini, summer squash, and bell peppers

¼ pound (115 g) any combination of onion, shallots, leeks, and gingerroot

½ pound (225 g) any combination of radishes, celery, beets, brussels sprouts, cauliflower, and carrots

1 or 2 cloves of garlic (optional)

1 tablespoon (18 g) kosher salt

2 cups (470 ml) filtered water

RANDOM PICKLE GENERATOR

Fermentation is flexible! Don't believe me? Try this recipe. All of the vegetables listed here ferment very well, especially when fermented in a mix. I haven't tested every possible iteration of this recipe, so I can't promise that you'll love them all, but most of the time, this is how I ferment for home use. What do I have in the produce drawer? I'll use that! What looks good at the market? Oh, I'll take three! I hope this encourages you to use what you already have at home to make healthful and delicious pickles.

Chop the zucchini, summer squash, and/or bell peppers into 1- to 2-inch (2.5 to 5 cm) thick strips. Peel and dice the onions and shallots, slice the leeks into ¼-inch (0.5 cm) rounds, and grate the ginger. Chop the radishes, celery, beets, brussels sprouts, cauliflower, and/or carrots into 1-inch (2.5 cm) pieces. Peel and halve the garlic cloves.

Place the garlic in the bottom of a quart (1 L) jar and place all the vegetables on top,
putting the smallest pieces on the bottom and the largest pieces on top.

Mix the salt into water until dissolved and pour the brine over the vegetables, ensuring that there is a thin layer of brine just covering the vegetables.

Using your preferred method (see pages 23 to 28), submerge your veggies and cover your jar.

Place your jar on a small plate or bowl and allow to ferment at room temperature for about 2 weeks.

Once you're happy with the flavor and acidity, remove the weight, secure the lid, and place the jar in the fridge. Enjoy chilled.

Yield: 1 quart (900 g)

SNAPPY PEA PICKLES

Snap peas are hard to ferment. Not because they're actually difficult, but because you have to not eat them all on your way home from the market if you want them to make it to the jar. I've learned to buy double what I think I'll need so that I can have a few pints going throughout the spring. Be sure to trim the ends—it keeps the peas crisp and reduces the odds of unsightly surface yeasts.

Zest of 1 lemon

Two 2-inch (5 cm) sprigs of garden mint

2 cups (150 g) snap peas, ends trimmed

1½ teaspoons (9 g) kosher salt

1 cup (235 ml) filtered water

Place the lemon zest and mint in the bottom of a pint (500 ml) jar and then add the snap peas.

Mix the salt into water until dissolved and pour this brine over the peas, ensuring that there is a thin layer of brine over the vegetables.

Using your preferred method (see pages 23 to 28), submerge your veggies and cover your jar.

Place your jar on a small plate or bowl and allow to ferment at room temperature for 5 days to 2 weeks.

Once you're happy with the flavor and acidity, remove the weight, secure the lid, and place the jar in the fridge. Enjoy chilled.

Yield: 1 pint (450 g)

RECIPE NOTE Like peppers, snap peas may have a bit more white sediment than other vegetables. That's normal and fine.

PICKLE MY JICAMA

Lovers of Mexican cuisine will know the fresh, juicy flavor of jicama well. I frequently pickle jicama with well-loved flavors of Mexico, including lime, garlic, radishes, and cilantro, so I was surprised when, on a whim, I subbed those seasonings out in favor of whole star anise. The warm baking spice turned out to be the perfect complement to the crisp, cool flesh of the jicama. Look for a thin-skinned vegetable with few blemishes for a primo pickle. If you can only find thicker-skinned jicama, it's fine to trim the peels off after fermentation.

1 small (¾ pound, 340 g) jicama

3 whole star anise

1½ teaspoons (9 g) kosher salt

1 cup (235 ml) filtered water

Cut any soft parts or blemishes from the outside of the jicama, but leave it otherwise unpeeled. Cut the jicama into ½ inch (1.5 cm) thick sticks.

Place the star anise in the bottom of a pint (500 ml) jar. Stand the jicama slices on end in the jar, pressing them together as necessary to fit the pieces into the jar.

Mix the salt into water until dissolved and pour this brine into the jar, ensuring that there is a thin layer of brine over the top of the jicama.

Using your preferred method (see pages 23 to 28), submerge your veggies and cover your jar.

Place your jar on a small plate or bowl and allow to ferment at room temperature for 1 to 2 weeks.

Once you're happy with the flavor and acidity, remove the weight, secure the lid, and place the jar in the fridge. Enjoy chilled.

Yield: 1 pint (450 g)

Ingredients

- 1 daikon, about 1 pound (450 g)
- 4 carrots, about 1 pound (450 g) total
- 4 teaspoons (23 g) kosher salt
- 1 jalapeño pepper
- 1½ cloves of garlic, peeled

BÁNH MÌ PICKLES

Although *bánh mì* actually means "bread" in Vietnamese, in the U.S., the term generally refers to the delightful sandwich that perfectly aligns many wonderful flavors and textures. Unsurprisingly, my favorite part of a bánh mì sandwich is the pickled mix of daikon and carrot that provides texture, moisture, and loads of flavor. This fermented version is nontraditional, with less sweetness and more flavor than the typical blend found in sandwich shops. If you want the sweeter version on your sandwich, toss the finished pickles with 2 teaspoons (12 g) of sugar per cup (225 g) just before serving.

Julienne the daikon and carrots. Place in a bowl and toss with the salt.

Slice the jalapeño lengthwise into two equal halves. Set it aside.

Thinly slice the garlic and toss it in with the root mixture.

After sitting with the salt for a short while, the carrots and daikon will have released some moisture. Take a small handful of the now damp vegetables and pack them into a quart (1 L) jar. Lay 1 jalapeño half cut-side against the side of the jar, push the pointed end into the vegetable mixture at the bottom of the jar, and pack the roots in around it. Once the pepper is held in place, put the other jalapeño half against another side of the jar and pack more daikon carrot mixture around it until all of the vegetables are in the jar and the jalapeño halves are pressed against the sides of the jar.

Press down on the vegetables in the jar to draw the maximum amount of brine to the surface.

Using your preferred method (see pages 23 to 28), submerge your veggies and cover your jar.

Place your jar on a small plate or bowl and allow to ferment at room temperature for 1 week or until the desired acidity is achieved.

Once you're happy with the flavor and acidity, remove the weight, secure the lid, and place the jar in the fridge.

Yield: 1 quart (900 g)

Vegetable A-peel

Although washing vegetables in cool water is great, peeling vegetables for fermentation is a no-no. The majority of the bacteria necessary for fermentation live on the skins of vegetables. A peeled vegetable may fail to ferment, or it may ferment extraordinarily slowly, leading to issues with texture or mold.

CURRIED CAULIFLOWER PICKLES

Cauliflower and curry are a classic combination for good reason. I like to serve these pickles alongside seasoned rice dishes or in winter salads (try them with dressed kale). This recipe is an exception to the no-powdered-spices-in-brine rule. The curry powder will mostly sit at the bottom of the jar, but its flavor will infuse throughout the brine during fermentation.

1 tablespoon (6.5 g) curry powder

½ head (12 ounces, or 340 g) cauliflower, chopped into small florets

1 tablespoon (18 g) kosher salt

2 cups (470 ml) filtered water, at room temperature

Place the curry powder in a quart (1 L) jar and then add the florets. The florets may need to be maneuvered a bit to fit, but don't push them so hard that they break apart.

Mix the salt into water until dissolved and pour the brine over the florets, pressing them down with clean fingers to make sure they're submerged. The jar should be full to about 1½ inches (4 cm) below the rim.

Using your preferred method (see pages 23 to 28), submerge your veggies and cover your jar.

Place your jar on a small plate or bowl and allow to ferment at room temperature for 10 days to 2 weeks. The texture of the cauliflower will remain largely unchanged.

Once you're happy with the flavor and acidity, remove the weight, secure the lid, and place the jar in the fridge.

Yield: 1 quart (900 g)

CURRIED CAULIFLOWER PICNIC SALAD ››

This is my go-to picnic potluck contribution. With the exception of the low-fat crowd, this is doable for just about any diet. If you're bringing it to a gathering with vegan friends, sub vegan mayo. If your friends are all paleo, consider a homemade version made with your favorite nut oil. Whichever mayo you use, this is a crowd-pleaser, and it never lasts long.

⅓ cup (75 g) mayonnaise

2 teaspoons (10 g) Dijon or sweet hot mustard

1 quart (900 g) Curried Cauliflower Pickles, drained

2 stalks of celery, trimmed and sliced crosswise

2 scallions, trimmed and sliced into thin rounds

Combine the mayonnaise and mustard in a large bowl. Add the cauliflower and toss to coat. Mix in the celery and scallions. Enjoy chilled.

Yield: 4 servings (1 cup [225 g] each)

Ingredients

½ small Italian eggplant (7 ounces, or 200 g), cut into ¼-inch (0.5 cm) slices

½ red bell pepper (3 ounces, or 75 g), stem, seeds, and pith removed

¼ large onion (2 ounces, or 60 g), peeled

2 teaspoons (2.5 g) whole-spice herbes de Provence

3 small zucchini (13 ounces, or 360 g), ends trimmed, cut into ¾-inch (2 cm) cubes

2 small yellow summer squash (8½ ounces, or 240 g), ends trimmed, cut into ¾-inch (2 cm) cubes

1½ tablespoons (27 g) kosher salt

3 cups (700 ml) filtered water

½ cup (20 g) fresh basil leaves, chopped, for garnish

RAW-TATOUILLE

This take on a famous taste of Provence makes use of the best end-of-summer vegetables. Unlike the cooked version, this raw ratatouille is loaded with probiotic bacteria and makes an excellent summer salad once chilled and drained. You can use your own combination of Mediterranean spices if you like, but the herbes de Provence spice blend called for in the recipe (a combination of savory, marjoram, rosemary, thyme, oregano, and sometimes lavender) will have you dreaming of whitewashed, cliff-side dwellings and blue seas.

Quarter the eggplant slices and chop the bell pepper and onion into 1-inch (2.5 cm) squares.

Place the herbes de Provence into a ½-gallon (2 L) jar (or split evenly between 2 quart [1 L] jars). Place all the vegetables in the jar.

Mix the salt into water until dissolved and pour the brine over the vegetables, ensuring that there is a thin layer of brine into the jar.

Using your preferred method (see pages 23 to 28), submerge your veggies and cover your jar.

Place your jar on a plate and allow to ferment at room temperature in a spot away from direct sunlight for 5 to 7 days. When ready, the vegetables should taste quite tangy, but the zucchini should still be crisp.

Once you're happy with the flavor and acidity, remove the weight, secure the lid, and place the jar in the fridge. Store in the brine, but drain and toss with the chopped basil before serving as a side dish.

Yield: 2 quarts (1.8 kg)

Ingredients

1 pound (450 g) hakurei
or other small turnips,
greens removed

1 tablespoon (18 g)
kosher salt

2 cups (470 ml)
filtered water

Three 3-inch (7.5 cm) sprigs of
fresh garden mint, for
use post-fermentation

MINTY HAKUREI TURNIPS

Hakurei turnips are the perfectly round, diminutive, white turnips that have taken farmers' markets across the country by storm in recent years. They hail from Japan and their flavor is milder than their larger turnip counterparts. They have a delightful, juicy crunch that lends itself perfectly to pickling. While mint may be an unexpected pairing, it makes for a truly refreshing pickle.

Trim and quarter the unpeeled turnips and place them in a quart (1 L) jar. There should be about an inch (2.5 cm) of space between the top of the vegetables and the rim of the jar.

Mix the salt into water until dissolved and pour the brine into the jar, ensuring that there is a thin layer of brine over the vegetables.

Using your preferred method (see pages 23 to 28), submerge your veggies and cover your jar.

Place your jar on a small plate or bowl and allow to ferment at room temperature, away from direct sunlight, for 1 to 2 weeks.

Once you're happy with the acidity, remove the weight and stick the mint springs into the jar, weighting them down with pickles. Secure the lid and place the jar in the fridge. After 3 days, you may remove the mint sprigs. Your minty turnips are ready to eat!

Yield: 1 quart (900 g)

Ingredients

1 turnip (½ pound, or 225 g)

1 small carrot (¼ pound, or 115 g)

1 teaspoon (2 g) caraway seeds

1 teaspoon (4 g) mustard seeds

1 teaspoon (6 g) salt

½ cup (120 ml) filtered water

CARROT CARAWAY TURNIP SLICES

If I had invented the deli, carrot turnip pickles would probably be the standard pickle. This works well as both a sandwich filling and a sandwich accompaniment. Line a slice of bread with a few of these babies and it pretty much doesn't matter what else you add.

Trim the top off of the turnip. Remove and discard any unattractive, soft, or rooty bits, but leave it otherwise unpeeled.

Cut the turnip and carrot into ¼-inch (0.5 cm) thick slices. If the turnip slices have a diameter wider than the diameter of the jar, simply cut them in half.

Place the caraway and mustard seeds in a pint (500 ml) jar and layer the turnip and carrot slices on top.

Mix the salt into water until dissolved and pour the brine into the jar, ensuring that there is a thin layer of brine over the vegetables.

Using your preferred method (see pages 23 to 28), submerge your veggies and cover your jar.

Place your jar on a small plate or bowl and allow to ferment at room temperature for 2 to 3 weeks.

Once you're happy with the flavor and acidity, remove the weight, secure the lid, and place the jar in the fridge.

Yield: 1 pint (450 g)

Ingredients

- 1 pound (450 g) asparagus
- 1 teaspoon (4 g) mustard seeds
- 3 cloves of garlic, peeled
- Peel (without pith) of ½ of a lemon
- 4 teaspoons (22 g) kosher salt
- 2 cups (475 ml) filtered water

ASPARAGUS PICKLES

When I spot local asparagus in the produce section, I know that the days of snuggies and stews are coming to an end. I always make an early spring batch of these pickles to reorient my taste buds to the cool, fresh flavors of warmer seasons. Look for medium-width asparagus spears that are roughly equal in size. Serve these as a side dish or as a beautiful bed for poached eggs at brunch.

Trim the woody ends off of the asparagus spears. Take one spear and stand it in a quart (900 g) jar. Its tip should fall 1 to 2 inches (2.5 to 5 cm) below the rim of the jar. If the spear is too tall, trim more, test again, and then trim all other pieces to match its length.

Place the mustard seeds, garlic, and lemon peel into a quart (1 L) jar and then fit the asparagus spears into the jar, standing the spears on end. Tilting the jar sideways will help you fit more spears in without damaging them. Do not cram or damage the spears. Smashed ends may lead to unpleasant sliminess.

Mix the salt into water until dissolved and pour this brine over the asparagus, ensuring that there is a thin layer of brine over the vegetables.

Using your preferred method (see pages 23 to 28), submerge your veggies and cover your jar.

Place your jar on a small plate or bowl and allow to ferment at room temperature for 5 days to 2 weeks.

Once you're happy with the flavor and acidity, remove the weight, secure the lid, and place the jar in the fridge. Enjoy chilled.

Yield: 1 quart (900 g)

Ingredients

- 1 small red bell pepper, stems, pith, and seeds removed
- 1 small green bell pepper, stems, pith, and seeds removed
- 2 cloves of garlic, peeled and roasted

  Zest of 1 lemon
- 1 teaspoon (3 g) capers
- 1 teaspoon (1.5 g) packed fresh oregano leaves (or ½ teaspoon [0.5 g] dried)

  Pinch of red pepper flakes (optional)
- 1 sprig of basil, left whole
- 2 teaspoons (12 g) kosher salt
- 1 cup (235 ml) filtered water

PINT OF PICKLED PEPPERS

The first time I made pickled peppers, I was pretty sad. It was early in my fermentation habit, and I had grown accustomed to a set, 2-week fermentation time resulting in flawless pickles of all kinds. When I cracked that pepper jar, they were very soft. They smelled incredible, so I took a bite (they tasted great), but that was when I learned that not all vegetables were created equal where fermentation is concerned and some require less time. I sometimes still ferment them for longer than 2 weeks, then toss them into salads or top pizzas with them, but for a crispy bell pepper, 5 to 6 days does the trick.

Slice the peppers into ½-inch (1.5 cm) strips. Place the garlic, lemon zest, capers, oregano, and red pepper flakes in a pint (500 ml) jar. Gently pack the pepper strips in, standing them on end to create a striped appearance when the jar is viewed. Alternating red and green slices makes for a pretty pickle.

Press the basil sprig into the middle of the peppers. This is a relatively short fermentation period, so you don't have to worry about it becoming mushy.

Mix the salt into water until dissolved and pour this brine over the peppers, ensuring that there is a thin layer of brine over the top of the radishes. A space should remain at the top of the jar once the brine has been added.

Using your preferred method (see pages 23 to 28), submerge your veggies and cover your jar.

Place your jar on a small plate or bowl and allow to ferment at room temperature for 5 to 6 days.

Once you're happy with the flavor and acidity, remove the weight, secure the lid, and place the jar in the fridge. Enjoy chilled.

Yield: 1 pint (450 g)

 Pepper pickle brine becomes quite cloudy during fermentation, so don't be concerned if this happens to yours.

Ingredients

½ large unwaxed rutabaga (12 ounces, or 340 g)

2 cloves of garlic, peeled and thinly sliced

2 teaspoons (12 g) kosher salt

Two 5-inch (13 cm) sprigs of fresh rosemary

ROSEMARY RUTABAGA

This simple combination was inspired by a dish I made for my very first Thanksgiving in California. At my Michigan family's feast, mashed rutabaga is *de rigueur.* My Californian in-laws weren't quite as attached to this underappreciated vegetable superstar, so I made it my business to convince them—using copious amounts of garlic and a few sprigs from the enormous rosemary bush that lived, year-round, outside my Monterey apartment. More than one of my new relatives was won over by the humble root that day, and now I make the dish whenever I visit for the holidays.

Trim the top off of the rutabaga. Remove and discard any unattractive, soft, or rooty bits, but leave it otherwise unpeeled.

Using a mandoline, if possible, cut the rutabaga into ¼ inch (0.5 cm) wide matchsticks. If prepping by hand, cut ¼-inch (0.5 cm) slices and then cut each slice into ¼-inch (0.5 cm) matchsticks.

In a large bowl, toss the garlic and rutabaga with the salt using clean hands. Continue tossing and gently squeeze the vegetables until they are damp and there is a small amount of liquid in the bottom of the bowl.

Pack a third of the rutabaga mixture into the bottom of a pint (500 ml) jar. Pack tightly, with clean fingers. Wrap one sprig of rosemary around the inside of the jar, as pictured. Pack another third of the rutabaga mixture on top and repeat with final third of rutabaga. Pour any liquid from the bowl into the jar.

Using your preferred method (see pages 23 to 28), submerge your veggies and cover your jar.

Place your jar on a small plate or bowl and allow to ferment at room temperature for 1 to 3 weeks.

Once you're happy with the flavor and acidity, remove the weight, secure the lid, and place the jar in the fridge. Enjoy chilled or at room temperature.

Yield: 1 pint (450 g)

Ingredients

- 1 pound (450 g) brussels sprouts, trimmed
- 5 cloves of garlic, peeled
- 20 hazelnuts, chopped
- 2 tablespoons (22 g) mustard seed
- 4 teaspoons (23 g) kosher salt
- 2 cups (470 ml) filtered water

NUTTY BRUSSELS SPROUT PICKLES

One of my very favorite ways to eat brussels sprouts is the braised and glazed sprouts from Mark Bittman's *How to Cook Everything*. I make the recipe exactly as directed right up until the end, when I add a bit of roasted garlic, some chopped hazelnuts, and a spoonful of mustard to finish them off. I love the flavors so much that I decided they would make an excellent pickle. They do! There's no need to get the skins off the hazelnuts. The fermentation process neutralizes the bitterness that you sometimes get when cooking or baking hazelnuts with the skin on. Brussels sprouts definitely fall into the stinky ferment camp, so be prepared for a bit of extra aroma.

Cut each brussels sprout in half lengthwise. Place the garlic, hazelnuts, and mustard seeds into a quart (1 L) jar. Top with the brussels sprout halves. You may need to maneuver the brussels sprouts so that they fit in the jar with 1 to 2 inches (2.5 to 5 cm) of space below the rim of the jar.

Mix the salt into water until dissolved and pour the brine into the jar, ensuring that there is a thin layer of brine over the vegetables.

Using your preferred method (see pages 23 to 28), submerge your veggies and cover your jar.

Place your jar on a small plate or bowl and allow to ferment at room temperature for 3 to 6 weeks or longer in colder months.

Once you're happy with the flavor and acidity, remove the weight, secure the lid, and place the jar in the fridge. Enjoy chilled.

Yield: 1 quart (900 g)

Ingredients

- 5 small zucchini, ends trimmed (1 pound, or 450 g)
- 1 large pinch of powdered nutmeg, preferably freshly ground
- 1 tablespoon (2 g) loose black tea, or 2 or 3 tea bags
- 2 tablespoons (15 g) coarsely chopped walnuts
- 2 cinnamon sticks
- 1 tablespoon (18 g) kosher salt
- 2 cups (470 ml) filtered water

ZUCCHINI BREAD PICKLES

I have an enduring love for zucchini bread that doesn't jive so well with my desire to avoid loads of processed sugar. So when my husband, Jake, suggested I try making a pickle version, I only called him crazy three times before I got to work on a recipe. This pickle isn't sweet, but it might just replace your sweet tooth with a sour one.

Cut the zucchini lengthwise into quarters.

Place the nutmeg, tea, walnuts, and cinnamon sticks into a quart (1 L) jar in that order. Fit the zucchini pieces into the jar, standing the spears on end.

Mix the salt into water until dissolved and pour the brine into the zucchini, ensuring that there is a thin layer of brine over the zucchini.

Using your preferred method (see pages 23 to 28), submerge your veggies and cover your jar.

Place your jar on a small plate or bowl and allow to ferment at room temperature in a spot away from direct sunlight for 4 days. Go a day shorter if your home is particularly warm or a day longer if your home is particularly cool.

Once you're happy with the flavor and acidity, remove the weight, secure the lid, and place the jar in the fridge for up to a week (or until they are no longer crisp). See "Cucumbers and Other Tricky Pickles" on page 69 for zucchini pickling tips.

Yield: 1 quart (900 g)

What to Do with a Floppy Pickle

Just because a ferment has gone soft in the back of the fridge doesn't mean it's ready for the compost pile. Softness might mean a ferment is past its prime from a texture standpoint, but it definitely doesn't mean it has no more to offer. Fermented pickles and their brines are loaded with flavor and acid, which makes them great candidates for culinary experimentation. Add them to soups or stews. Strain and purée them into dips or sauces. Your imagination is the only limit on the second life of these kitchen heroes.

RECIPE NOTES

Variations: Add the zest of 1 small lemon and 2 teaspoons of dried sage leaves to the jar before adding the sweet potatoes for fermentation. Discard the seasonings before frying.

For baked nests: Toss the drained sweet potatoes with 1 to 2 tablespoons (15 to 30 ml) of olive or melted coconut oil. Separate into nests and bake them on parchment paper at 400°F (200°C, or gas mark 6) for 15 minutes or until crispy.

Ingredients

1	large sweet potato (2 pounds, or 900 g), spiralized, skin on
4½	teaspoons (28 g) kosher salt
1½	cups (355 ml) filtered water
1	quart (940 ml) high-heat oil

SWEET POTATO FRY NESTS

A French chef once explained to me that although he prided himself on from-scratch cooking, he never made fries in-house. "It's impossible to do them right in a kitchen this size," he said. He went on to explain that the only way to get a really great French fry was to soak the potatoes for at least 36 hours before frying. Essentially, all great fries (like all great food, in my biased opinion) are fermented before they're fried. The fermentation process eliminates the risk of a harmful compound called acrylamide from forming during cooking and greatly improves the texture of the final fries. There are two options here, baked and deep-fried. Unsurprisingly, the fried version is greatly preferred by my friends and family, but the baked version does come out crispy and better than the vast majority of restaurant shoestring fries you'll ever order. And like any great French fry, this is definitely not health food. Enjoy with ketchup or poached eggs and kale.

Place the sweet potatoes in a quart (1 L) jar.

Mix the salt into water until dissolved and pour the brine into the jar, ensuring that there is a thin layer of brine over the sweet potatoes.

Using your preferred method (see pages 23 to 28), submerge your veggies and cover your jar.

Place your jar on a small plate or bowl and allow to ferment at room temperature for 5 to 7 days.

Drain the liquid from the sweet potatoes and spread them out in a single layer on a large kitchen towel. Pat dry.

Pour the oil into a 3-quart (2.7 L), heavy-bottomed pot and heat to 400°F (200°C). While you're waiting for the oil to heat, continue patting the sweet potatoes dry. Pull them apart and pile them up so that each long strand becomes a little nest. There will be a few odds and ends. Those can be made into their own piles of similar size to the single-strand nests.

Line a platter with paper towels.

Once the oil temperature hits 400°F (200°C), it's time to start frying. Working in batches, use a spoon to lower each nest into the oil. Fry 3 or 4 nests at a time to avoid overcrowding. Fry for 45 seconds to 1 minute. If they've started browning, they've gone too long. Use a slotted spoon to remove them and place them on the paper towels.

Allow the temperature to return to 400°F (200°C) before frying the next batch. Repeat until all of the potatoes have been fried. The oil can be reused for other purposes for several days.

Yield: Approximately 20 fry nests

COCKTAIL ONION RINGS

The classic pearl onions pickled for cocktail use can be a pain in the allium to peel. I avoid that problem by making these onion "rings" instead. They fit nicely in a martini glass and require much less effort. Teetotalers can enjoy these piled high on a burger or sandwich.

2 medium-small onions (5½ ounces, or 150 g each), peeled

8 juniper berries

2 allspice berries

Peel of 1 lemon

1 tablespoon (5 g) peppercorns

2 bay leaves

3-inch (7.5 cm) sprig of fresh thyme

1½ teaspoons (9 g) kosher salt

1 cup (235 ml) filtered water

Cut the onions into ½-inch (1.5 cm) slices.

Place the seasonings into a wide-mouth pint (500 ml) jar and stack the onion slices on top of them, filling the jar to 1½ inches (4 cm) below the rim.

Mix the salt into water until dissolved and pour the brine into the jar, ensuring that there is a thin layer of brine over the onions.

Using your preferred method (see pages 23 to 28), submerge your veggies and cover your jar.

Place your jar on a small plate or bowl and allow to ferment at room temperature for 1 to 2 weeks.

Once you're happy with the flavor and acidity, remove the weight, secure the lid, and place the jar in the fridge.

Yield: 1 pint (450 g)

RECIPE NOTE The onions for this recipe should be chosen for their diameter (slices need to be able to stack inside the jar). If your widest onion slice is a little too wide, just remove an outer ring and use it for another purpose.

DIRTY GIBSON ››

When life (or your own handy kitchen skills) gives you pickled onions, make gin drinks! Will drinking this make you healthier, wealthier, or wiser? Nope! But it will make your taste buds sing.

1 or 2 Cocktail Onion Rings

4 teaspoons (20 ml) brine from Cocktail Onion Rings

2½ ounces (75 ml) gin

¾ teaspoon (4 ml) dry vermouth

Place the onion rings in a martini glass. Shake the brine, gin, and vermouth with ice in a cocktail shaker and strain into a glass. Serve chilled.

Yield: 1 cocktail

Ingredients

- 1 pound (450 g) freshly picked Kirby cucumbers
- 1 tablespoons (11 g) mustard seeds
- 1 bulb of garlic, peeled
- 2 teaspoons (3.5 g) peppercorns
- 4 dill heads or ½ a bunch of fresh dill
- 4 grape leaves
- 1 tablespoon (18 g) kosher salt
- 2 cups (470 ml) filtered water

CLASSIC DILL PICKLE SPEARS

It is pretty hard to beat a deli pickle. These flavors can be a gateway to a whole world of fermented fun. Believe it or not, though, the classic pickle is one of the most difficult to make. Follow the tips and tricks on the next page, and you'll do just fine.

Wash the cukes well and soak them in ice water for 30 minutes. This tends to help them stay firm during fermentation.

Remove and discard a very thin slice from each end of the cucumbers. Cut the cucumbers into long quarters.

Place the mustard seeds, garlic, peppercorns, dill heads, and grape leaves into a quart (1 L) jar and add the cucumber spears.

Mix the salt into water until dissolved and pour this brine over the cucumbers, ensuring that there is a thin layer of brine over the vegetables.

Using your preferred method (see pages 23 to 28), submerge your veggies and cover your jar.

Place your jar on a small plate or bowl and allow to ferment at room temperature for 3 days.

Remove the weight, secure the lid, and place the jar in the fridge. Allow the flavors to infuse for another week before eating. Once they're ready, enjoy within 2 weeks for best texture.

Yield: 1 quart (900 g)

Cucumbers and Other Tricky Pickles

Cucumbers are easily the most iconic vegetable to pickle. And yet, they're probably the most difficult vegetable to ferment! Here are a few simple tricks that will have you making perfect cucumber pickles every time. These tips also help with zucchini (Zucchini Bread Pickles, page 63), summer squash, and other soft vegetables.

- **Keep it short.** With most vegetable fermentation, timing is relative. The longer it ferments, the more sour it will be, so it becomes a matter of preference. With soft vegetables like cucumbers, however, the shorter timing recommendations in each recipe should be more strictly observed; otherwise, you may open up a jar of mush instead of a gorgeous, crispy pickle.

- **Try tannins.** Mushy texture and hollow pickle syndrome are common problems that arise when pickling cucumbers. One way to help prevent these issues is to add tannins. Tannins (see page 160) help strengthen the pectins in the vegetables and keep pickles crispy!

- **Remove the blossom end.** The blossom end, or the non-stem end, of a cucumber is a safe haven for the kinds of enzymes that cause food to rot. Removing the tiniest sliver of the blossom end removes some of those enzymes, resulting in a crisper pickle and one less likely to turn to mush.

- **Go small.** Smaller is better when it comes to cucumber fermentation, and don't even bother trying to ferment slicers. Stick to the smallest Kirbys (small pickling cucumbers) you can find.

- **Season freely.** Perhaps it's because they're often left whole during fermentation, but cucumber pickles require more seasoning than other pickled vegetables. Where I might use a couple cloves of garlic for a beet pickle, I'd use a bulb for a cucumber pickle. This is true for herbs and spices as well.

- **Ferment the harvest.** The freshness of the cucumber is probably the most important consideration on this list. Don't bother with grocery store cucumbers; grow them yourself or buy them from a farmers' market and make sure that you get them submerged in brine as soon as you can. Even a few days off the vine can make for a hollow or soft pickle.

- **Eat 'em up.** Most fermented vegetables will easily last for months in the fridge (not that you'll be able to resist them for that long!). Cucumber pickles will occasionally keep for two or more months (I once found a perfect jar a year after fermentation!), but more commonly, you'll want to eat them quickly, while they still have the best, crisp bite.

Kraut

I live in the real world. I know that, although few things make my mouth water more than the thought of cracking into a jar of this classic fermented food, the idea of fermented cabbage can be challenging for the uninitiated. Those who've joined the clan of kraut makers, though, know that "fermented" is synonymous with "delicious."

For fermenters who like to experiment, sauerkraut can be a blank canvas on which to paint a picture as simple or as complex as you like. A jar of the Simplest Sauerkraut (page 76) is anything but plain. The acids and other compounds created during fermentation give it an enormous amount of distinctive flavor, even though no seasonings have been added. When you do add seasonings, you can take sauerkraut in directions that may initially seem surprising (Sauerkraut Satay, page 90). The power of fermentation somehow manages to bring it all together beautifully. It is no exaggeration to say that sauerkraut can be enjoyed at every meal, including dessert (Carrot Cake Kraut, page 98).

Tips and Guidelines

The general principles of fermentation laid out in part one apply to the recipes in this chapter, but here are a few sauerkraut-specific tips and guidelines.

Choosing the Cabbage

Red, green, and savoy are only a fraction of your cabbage options. Here in Pennsylvania (otherwise know as American Kraut Country), farmers' markets sometimes offer such a wide variety of heirloom cabbages that it can get overwhelming. I have yet to ferment a cabbage that didn't make delectable kraut, but the varying water content and leaf density of different varieties can make for a slightly different final product. Red cabbage, for instance, takes a bit longer to ferment to that classic kraut texture than green does. It's nothing to be concerned with. If you see a beautiful cabbage that you really want to use, do it, and glory in the minor differences that make that batch unique.

Cutting the Cabbage

For some people, the act of chopping cabbage for sauerkraut is a moment of Zen in a hectic world—a way to unwind with some hands-on interaction. If that's you, go nuts. Have some large bowls and a very sharp chef's knife on hand. Cut out the core, remove any wilted outer leaves, and shoot for strips that are relatively uniform and about ¼ inch (0.5 cm) wide.

For the lazy among us (that's me!), there are food processors with slicing and grating blades, box graters, mandolines, and even specialized cabbage shredders made for this express purpose. Do what works best for you.

With few exceptions, the cabbage in this chapter was shredded using the slicer blade on my food processor, into approximately ¼-inch (0.5 cm) wide strips. Recipes that were grated will be noted as such in the recipe. The salting process drains water from the cabbage and shrinks it significantly as a result. If you choose to grate your cabbage where I've sliced it, know that smaller pieces ferment a bit more quickly, so you might want to start tasting for your preferred acidity level a week or so earlier than the recipe calls for. Smaller pieces also take up less jar space and absorb seasonings more readily, so add a couple more ounces (15 to 30 g) of cabbage and reduce the seasonings a bit if you decide to adapt the recipes this way.

You can also opt to leave the hard cabbage core in the ferment if you'd like, but those pieces ferment more slowly than the rest of the cabbage, so be prepared for some divergent textures and acidity levels within your kraut.

If you want a more uniform kraut but don't want to compost the cores, slice them thin and ferment them separately in brine as cabbage core pickles.

Saving the Leaves

When you're prepping your head of cabbage, be sure to remove any outer leaves that are a bit wilted and less than lovely. See the "How to Make a Cabbage Shelf" (page 75) for how to put them to good use.

Massaging the Cabbage

Treat your cabbage to a spa day! Gently massaging your cabbage after salting helps the salt penetrate the cell walls and increases the speed with which the cabbage gives up its internal water. When you salt the cabbage, toss well for even distribution and then leave it alone for 20 minutes or so while you prepare your other ingredients. When you come back, the salted cabbage will be more pliable—relaxed, high on incense fumes, and listening to the sweet melodies of the pan flute while it awaits the gentle pressure of your hands that will transform it into a jar-ready substance.

Packing a Jar or Crock

Packing your vessel is one of the most important steps. When approached properly, you should look at the bowl of salted cabbage and think, "There is no *way* all that cabbage is going to fit into that jar."

Working with small handfuls to start, carefully pack the cabbage into the jar so that its liquid rises to the top. Once you have the jar about one-third full, press down on the jarred cabbage with a flat fist. Holding your fist there, use your other hand to pour the cabbage liquid out of the jar. That will give you room to add more cabbage.

Adding Seasonings

Unlike brined pickles, sauerkraut adores powdered spices. You'll likely lose a bit of seasoning, be it whole or powdered spices, in the extra brine that results from salting and never makes it into your jar, and that's all right. You can mitigate that by draining the excess liquid off after massaging, but prior to mixing the seasonings in. Reserve that drained liquid, though. You may need to pour some of it back into your jar as a liquid barrier once all of the cabbage is packed inside.

Pouring liquid out makes room for more cabbage.

Fermenting Conditions

Sauerkraut generally benefits from a longer and cooler fermentation time. Although it will be safe to eat after just a few days of room temperature fermentation, it doesn't reach peak flavor and texture until several weeks have passed. I encourage you to taste frequently during your first attempt to find out what your preference is. Sauerkraut becomes more sour the longer it ferments.

Bubbling

Your sauerkraut will bubble vigorously in the early days, but that activity will slow as the predominant bacteria population shifts. This is normal and good. Just because it isn't bubbling vigorously does not mean that fermentation has stopped.

How to Make a Cabbage Shelf

Those less-than-perfect outer cabbage leaves you set aside are good for more than the compost pile. That sturdy rib makes a great shelf for your chosen fermentation weight, and the leafy part around it can be tucked down around the sides of your kraut or piled up and pressed down on top of the rib, creating a layer that protects the surface of your sauerkraut from any surface yeasts that could form.

To make your shelf, simply tear away the outer edges of a leaf until you're left with a piece that is roughly twice as large as your jar opening. Press the rib onto the top of the cabbage and tuck the leafy ends down around the sides of the kraut. Pour some of the remaining brine over the top of the leaf, leaving 1½ to 2 inches (4 to 5 cm) of space between the surface of the brine and the rim of the jar.

When the kraut tastes sour enough, you can discard the leaf and refrigerate the kraut.

Ingredients

2 pounds (900 g) cabbage

4 teaspoons (22 g) kosher salt

SIMPLEST SAUERKRAUT

In its simplest form, sauerkraut has just two ingredients: salt and cabbage. Consider this recipe the jumping-off point for all other recipes in this chapter. Use it to gain an understanding of the simplicity of the process and the fact that everything else is optional. Tasting a two-ingredient kraut can give you a serious appreciation for the immense amount of flavor that comes from the fermentation process alone.

Remove any unattractive or wilted outer leaves from the cabbage. Keep one handy. Cut out the core and rinse the cabbage in cool water.

Shred the cabbage into ¼-inch (0.5 cm) wide strips using a sharp chef's knife, the slicer blade of your food processor, a mandoline, or a kraut shredder.

Place the shredded cabbage into a large bowl, add the salt, and toss thoroughly for about 30 seconds or until the cabbage has a sheen of moisture on it. The salt has successfully drawn some water from the cabbage.

You now have the option of continuing to gently massage and squeeze the cabbage or letting the salt and cabbage continue osmosis while you go do something else for 20 minutes. If you let it sit a bit, the work of kneading the cabbage to release as much water as possible will be easier when you return.

Work it for another few minutes. When there is a visible puddle of water in the bottom of the bowl and the cabbage pieces stay in a clump when squeezed (as pictured), you are ready to start packing your jar.

Take a handful of cabbage in your dominant hand and a clean quart (1 L) jar in the other. Press the cabbage into the bottom of the jar and pack it along the bottom with the top of your fist or your fingers. Continue packing in this fashion, pressing along the sides and bottom, until it comes to about 1½ to 2 inches (4 to 5 cm) below the jar rim.

If there's still cabbage that hasn't been packed into the jar, press down on the top of the cabbage in the jar and tilt it to pour the cabbage liquid back into the bowl. This will give you more space in which to pack the remaining cabbage.

Use the cabbage leaf you reserved to create a "cabbage shelf" (see "How to Make a Cabbage Shelf," page 75). Pour the cabbage liquid from the bowl into the jar to cover the cabbage. Leave at least 1 inch (2.5 cm) of headspace at the top of the jar. Using your preferred method (see pages 23 to 28), weight the cabbage down and cover your jar.

Place your jar on a small plate or bowl and allow the kraut to ferment at room temperature for 2 to 6 weeks, depending on the warmth of your home. Check weekly to make sure that the brine level is still above the top of the cabbage. If it isn't, press down on your weight to get the brine to rise back above. If the brine is severely depleted, you may want to add more, at a concentration of about 5 percent (see salt charts on page 200), but there shouldn't be a need to do this.

Once you're happy with the acidity, remove the weight, secure the lid, and place the jar in the fridge.

Yield: 1 quart (900 g)

Ingredients

1½ pounds (675 g) green cabbage

½ pound (225 g) red cabbage

4 teaspoons (22 g) kosher salt

1 teaspoon (2 g) cumin seeds

2 teaspoons (7 g) mustard seeds

3 juniper berries

AVA'S HOT PINK KRAUT

Cooking with kids is a great way to get them interested in making healthier choices. My extended family does not always share my enthusiasm for fermented vegetables, so I recruited my niece, Ava, to help me make a version that would please her palate and cater to her love of the color pink. I'm not sure her mom was super happy when I handed her my chef's knife to remove the core, but my niece sure had fun squeezing the cabbage.

Remove any unattractive or wilted outer leaves from the cabbage, reserving one. Cut out the core and rinse the cabbage. Shred the cabbage into ¼-inch (0.5 cm) wide strips. Place in a large bowl, add the salt, and toss thoroughly for about 30 seconds or until the cabbage has a sheen of moisture on it.

Gently massage and squeeze the cabbage, or let it sit for a bit, to make the work easier, until there is a visible puddle of water in the bottom of the bowl and the cabbage pieces stay in a clump when squeezed.

Add the cumin and mustard seeds to the mix and continue tossing and massaging the cabbage.

Place the juniper berries into a clean quart (1 L) jar and then pack the mixture. First, pack it along the bottom using the top of your fist or your fingers. Continue packing in this fashion, pressing along the sides and bottom, until it comes to 1½ to 2 inches (4 to 5 cm) below the rim. If you need more space, press down on the cabbage and tilt the jar to pour cabbage liquid back into the bowl.

Use the reserved cabbage leaf to create a "cabbage shelf" (see page 75). Pour the cabbage liquid from the bowl into the jar to cover the cabbage. Leave 1½ to 2 inches (4 to 5 cm) of headspace at the top of the jar. Using your preferred method (see pages 23 to 28), weight the cabbage down and cover your jar.

Red cabbage juice is a beautiful, vibrant purple that will stain just about anything, so place your jar on a small plate or in a small plastic bag for the duration of fermentation. On the off chance that your jar bubbles over, stains won't be a concern.

Allow to ferment at room temperature for 3 to 4 weeks. Check weekly to make sure that the brine level is still above the top of the cabbage. If it isn't, press down on your weight to get the brine to rise back above.

Once you're happy with the acidity, remove the weight, secure the lid, and place the jar in the fridge.

Yield: 1 quart (900 g)

Ava's Kraut at 1 day (left) and 2 weeks (right).

Ingredients

2 pounds (900 g) cabbage

4 teaspoons (22 g) kosher salt

1 small onion (100 g), diced

3 stalks of celery, trimmed and diced

1 tablespoon (4.5 g) dried thyme

4 teaspoons (2.3 g) dried sage leaves

STUFFING KRAUT

When a dear friend was diagnosed with celiac disease shortly before our annual holiday party, I immediately went to work to make sure she could still have some of her favorite gluten-y flavors, while avoiding the serious health complications. This stuffing substitute does the trick.

Remove any unattractive or wilted outer leaves from the cabbage, reserving one. Cut out the core and rinse the cabbage. Shred the cabbage into ¼-inch (0.5 cm) wide strips. Place in a large bowl, add the salt, and toss thoroughly for about 30 seconds or until the cabbage has a sheen of moisture on it.

Gently massage and squeeze the cabbage, or let it sit for a bit, to make the work easier, until there is a visible puddle of water in the bottom of the bowl and the cabbage pieces stay in a clump when squeezed. Add the onion, celery, thyme, and sage and mix to distribute evenly.

Pack the mixture into a clean quart (1 L) jar. Pack it along the bottom using the top of your fist or your fingers. Continue packing in this fashion until it comes to 1½ to 2 inches (4 to 5 cm) below the rim. If there's still cabbage that hasn't been packed into the jar yet, press down on the top of the cabbage in the jar and tilt it to pour the cabbage liquid back into the bowl. This will give you more space in which to pack the remaining cabbage.

Use the reserved cabbage leaf to create a "cabbage shelf" (see page 75). Pour the cabbage liquid from the bowl into the jar to cover the cabbage. Leave 1 to 1½ inches (2.5 to 4 cm) of headspace at the top of the jar. Using your preferred method (see pages 23 to 28), weight the cabbage down and cover your jar.

Place your jar on a small plate or bowl and allow to ferment at room temperature for 2 to 4 weeks. Check weekly to make sure that the brine level is still above the top of the cabbage. If it isn't, press down on your weight to get the brine to rise back above.

Once you're happy with the acidity, remove the weight, secure the lid, and place the jar in the fridge.

Yield: 1 quart (900 g)

Ingredients

- 2 pounds (900 g) green cabbage
- 1 tablespoon (18 g) kosher salt
- 1 bulb of garlic, peeled and roasted until soft but not browned

KRAUTY THE VAMPIRE SLAYE[R]

Garlic lovers, this one's for you! This recipe is incredibly simple[,] step of roasting the garlic is what makes this kraut special. Ferme[nt] mellows the garlic substantially, so even the garlic *likers* in your fami[ly] will want to get their hands on this roasty, complex, and imperially garlic[ky] sauerkraut. Don't judge it by its early days; after just 2 weeks of fermentatio[n,] this kraut will lose the garlic pungency and gain a wonderful depth of flavor. If you intend to ferment for 4 to 6 weeks, add ½ a bulb more of garlic. One bulb works great for a 2- to 4-week fermentation period.

Remove any unattractive or wilted outer leaves from the cabbage, reserving one. Cut out the core and rinse the cabbage.

Grate the cabbage into a large bowl and add the salt. Gently massage and squeeze the cabbage, or let it sit for a bit to make the work easier, until there is a visible puddle of water in the bottom of the bowl and the cabbage pieces stay in a clump when squeezed.

Break the roasted garlic cloves into pieces and drop them into the cabbage mixture. Toss and knead the mixture, distributing the garlic as evenly as possible.

Pack the kraut into a clean quart (1 L) jar. First, pack it along the bottom using the top of your fist or your fingers. Continue packing in this fashion, pressing along the sides and bottom, until it comes to 1½ to 2 inches (4 to 5 cm) below the rim. If you need more space, press down on the cabbage and tilt the jar to pour the cabbage liquid back into the bowl.

Use the reserved cabbage leaf to create a "cabbage shelf" (see page 75). Pour the cabbage liquid from the bowl into the jar to cover the cabbage. Leave 1 to 1½ inches (2.5 to 4 cm) of headspace at the top of the jar. Using your preferred method (see pages 23 to 28), weight the cabbage down and cover your jar.

Place your jar on a small plate or bowl and allow to ferment at room temperature for 2 to 6 weeks. Check weekly to make sure that the brine level is still above the top of the cabbage. If it isn't, press down on your weight to bring some brine up to the top.

Once you're happy with the acidity, remove the weight, secure the lid, and place the jar in the fridge. Enjoy chilled.

Yield: 1 quart (900 g)

...OSE YOUR OWN ADVENTURE KRAUT

... make this kraut, the power is yours! Hate onions? Leave them out.
...ices? Don't bother! Have nothing in your fridge but a celery stalk,
...t, and a lemon slice? Use them up. Follow your own path to an
...nd tasty blend of fermented vegetables.

2 tablespoons (20 g) peeled
and diced onion, garlic,
shallot, or leek

4 teaspoons (22 g)
kosher salt

3 teaspoons total of any
of the following, combined
or alone: cumin seeds,
caraway seeds, allspice,
curry powder, juniper
berries, rubbed sage,
fresh thyme, red pepper
flakes, powdered ginger,
lemon zest, paprika,
or cayenne

...ny unattractive or wilted outer leaves from the cabbage, reserving one.
...e core and rinse the cabbage. Shred the cabbage into ¼-inch (0.5 cm)
...s.

... ther vegetables into ¼-inch (0.5 cm) slices. Place the vegetables into a
large bowl. Add the onion component and salt. Toss vigorously to evenly distribute
the salt. Add the herbs and spices and distribute them while massaging and tossing the cabbage with your hands.

Gently massage and squeeze the cabbage, or let it sit for a bit, to make the work
easier, until there is a visible puddle of water in the bottom of the bowl and the
cabbage pieces stay in a clump when squeezed.

Pack the mixture into a clean quart (1 L) jar. First, pack it along the bottom using
the top of your fist or your fingers. Continue packing in this fashion until it comes
to 1 to 1½ inches (2.5 to 4 cm) below the rim. If you need more space, press down
on the cabbage and tilt the jar to pour the cabbage liquid back into the bowl.

Use the reserved cabbage leaf to create a "cabbage shelf" (see page 75). Pour
the cabbage liquid from the bowl into the jar to cover the cabbage. Leave 1 to
1½ inches (2.5 to 4 cm) of headspace at the top of the jar. Using your preferred
method (see pages 23 to 28), weight the cabbage down and cover your jar.

Place your jar on a small plate or bowl and allow to ferment at room temperature
for 2 to 4 weeks. Check weekly to make sure that the brine level is still above the
top of the cabbage. If it isn't, press down on your weight to get the brine to rise
back above.

Once you're happy with the acidity, remove the weight, secure the lid, and place
the jar in the fridge.

Yield: 1 quart (900 g)

Ingredients

- 2 cups (500 g) Krauty the Vampire Slayer (page 81)

- 2 carrots, trimmed and julienned

- ½ red or yellow bell pepper, chopped

- ¼ cup (40 g) thinly sliced red onion

- 2 cups (150 g) snap peas, trimmed and cut lengthwise into thin strips

- 2 inches (5 cm) of peeled finely minced ginger

- 1 packed tablespoon (6 g) fresh mint, sliced into ribbons

- 2 packed tablespoons (2 g) chopped fresh cilantro

- 1 tablespoon (15 ml) toasted sesame oil

- 2 teaspoons (5.5 g) sesame seeds (optional)

SAUERKRAUT SLAW

My friend Sarah has always been avant-garde in her food habits. Long before anyone else I knew, she auditioned vegan and macrobiotic diets and cooked with locally grown products over grocery store fare. As a college sophomore, she was an expert at exploring the flavors of other cultures and making them American-teenager compatible. Although Asian-style slaws are common now, when Sarah first made one for me, I was extraordinarily excited by the new-to-me flavor combinations. This kraut-based slaw is an ode to the raw cabbage version she used to make in the kitchen of our shared college home.

Place the kraut, carrots, bell pepper, onion, snap peas, and ginger in a bowl. Toss to combine. Add the herbs and sesame oil and toss to coat. Sprinkle the sesame seeds on top and serve. This stores very well in the fridge, but the flavors have the best balance when served fresh.

Yield: 6 servings

Ingredients

1¾ pounds (790 g) cabbage

4 teaspoons (22 g)
kosher salt

4 or 5 hot peppers
(½ pound, or 225 g)

HEAT-LOVER'S KRAUT

You can use any hot peppers you like to make this particular sauerkraut. I like Hungarian wax, serrano, and jalapeño. This combination of green and yellow peppers makes a pretty kraut, but better yet, the fermentation process tames the heat of the peppers just a touch so you get a ton of the character in every smokin' bite.

Remove any unattractive or wilted outer leaves from the cabbage, reserving one. Cut out the core and rinse the cabbage. Shred the cabbage into ¼-inch (0.5 cm) wide strips. Place in a large bowl, add the salt, and toss thoroughly for about 30 seconds or until the cabbage has a sheen of moisture on it.

Gently massage and squeeze the cabbage, or let it sit for a bit, to make the work easier, until there is a visible puddle of water in the bottom of the bowl and the cabbage pieces stay in a clump when squeezed.

Remove and discard the crowns from the peppers. Slice it into thin rounds. Add the peppers to the cabbage bowl and toss with your hands to distribute. Hot peppers can actually be hot on the hands, so wear some disposable latex or brand-new dishwashing gloves to avoid a painful burning sensation.

Pack the mixture into a clean quart (1 L) jar. First, pack it along the bottom using the top of your fist or your fingers. Continue packing in this fashion, pressing along the sides and bottom, until it comes to 1½ to 2 inches (4 to 5 cm) below the rim. If you need more space, press down on the cabbage and tilt the jar to pour the cabbage liquid back into the bowl.

Use the reserved cabbage leaf to create a "cabbage shelf" (see page 75). Pour the cabbage liquid from the bowl into the jar to cover the cabbage. Leave 1 to 1½ inches (2.5 to 4 cm) of headspace at the top of the jar. Using your preferred method (see pages 23 to 28), weight the cabbage down and cover your jar.

Place your jar on a small plate or bowl and allow to ferment at room temperature for 3 to 4 weeks. Check weekly to make sure that the brine level is still above the top of the cabbage. If it isn't, press down on your weight to get the brine to rise back above.

Once you're happy with the acidity, remove the weight, secure the lid, and place the jar in the fridge.

Yield: 1 quart (900 g)

Ingredients

- 1 small unwaxed rutabaga (7 ounces, or 200 g), coarsely chopped
- 1 medium beet (7 ounces, or 200 g), coarsely chopped
- ½ head red cabbage (18 ounces, or 500 g)
- 4 teaspoons (22 g) kosher salt
- ⅓ cup (21 g) chopped fresh dill

DILLY ROOT KRAUT

As an American of Polish and Ukrainian descent, I am legally required to crave dill and root vegetables. Eating this kraut is like coming home. If you're willing to kill the good bugs, add this to borscht for a special treat.

Remove any unattractive or wilted outer leaves from the cabbage, reserving one. Cut out the core and rinse the cabbage. Shred the cabbage into ¼-inch (0.5 cm) wide strips. Place the vegetables in a large bowl, add the salt, and toss thoroughly for about 30 seconds or until the cabbage has a sheen of moisture on it.

Gently massage and squeeze the cabbage, or let it sit for a bit, to make the work easier, until there is a visible puddle of water in the bottom of the bowl and the cabbage pieces stay in a clump when squeezed. Add the dill and toss to distribute evenly.

Pack the mixture into a clean quart (1 L) jar. First, pack it along the bottom using the top of your fist or your fingers. Continue packing in this fashion, pressing along the sides and bottom, until it comes to 1½ to 2 inches (4 to 5 cm) below the rim. If you need more space, press down on the cabbage and tilt the jar to pour the cabbage liquid back into the bowl.

Use the reserved cabbage leaf to create a "cabbage shelf" (see page 75). Pour the cabbage liquid from the bowl into the jar to cover the cabbage. Leave 1 to 1½ inches (2.5 to 4 cm) of headspace at the top of the jar. Using your preferred method (see pages 23 to 28), weight the veggies down and cover your jar.

Red cabbage juice is a beautiful, vibrant purple that will stain just about anything, so place your jar on a small plate or in a small plastic bag during fermentation. Allow the cabbage to ferment at room temperature for 3 to 4 weeks. Check weekly to make sure that the brine level is still above the top of the cabbage. If it isn't, press down on your weight to get the brine to rise back above.

Once you're happy with the acidity, remove the weight, secure the lid, and place the jar in the fridge.

Yield: 1 quart (900 g)

Ingredients

- 1½ pounds (675 g) cabbage
- ½ red bell pepper
- 2 teaspoons (12 g) kosher salt
- ¼ cup (43 g) pitted kalamata or other Greek olives
- 1 clove of garlic, peeled
- 2 tablespoons (17 g) capers
- Four ⅛-inch (3 mm) slices of eggplant, the same diameter as the jar
- 2 ounces (55 g) of brined feta cheese (Do not use pre-crumbled.)

MEDITERRANEAN KRAUT

Move over, Greek salad. Your probiotic cousin is here to knock you off your lunch pedestal. This kraut is healthy and filling and makes a fantastic meal all on its own. Roll it up in a collard green for a gluten-free wrap or dig into it with oven-crisped pita chips. The vegetables are less salted here because several of the ingredients (the olives, capers, and cheese) already contain salt.

Remove any unattractive or wilted outer leaves from the cabbage and reserve one. Cut out and discard the core and rinse the cabbage. Shred the cabbage into ¼-inch (0.5 cm) wide strips. Place in a large bowl.

Remove the stem, seeds, and pith from the bell pepper and slice it into ½-inch (1.5 cm) squares. Place in the bowl with the cabbage. Add the salt and toss thoroughly for about 30 seconds or until the cabbage has a sheen of moisture on it.

Gently massage and squeeze the cabbage, or let it sit for a bit, to make the work easier, until there is a visible puddle of water in the bottom of the bowl and the cabbage pieces stay in a clump when squeezed.

Chop the olives and cut the garlic into thin slices. Add the olives, garlic, and capers to the cabbage bowl and toss well. Crumble the feta into the mix and toss lightly to distribute.

Pack roughly 1 cup (225 g) of the cabbage mixture into the bottom of a clean quart (1 L) jar. First, pack it along the bottom using the top of your fist or your fingers. Lay 1 slice of eggplant flat on top of it. Add another cup (225 g) of cabbage, packing tightly, and another eggplant slice. Repeat until the jar is full to about 1 inch (2.5 cm) from the top, ending with an eggplant slice.

Pour a bit of the remaining brine from the bowl over the top of the eggplant slice, still ensuring at least ¾-inch (2 cm) of headspace. Using your preferred method (see pages 23 to 28), weight the veggies down and cover your jar.

Place your jar on a small plate or bowl and allow to ferment at room temperature for 2 to 4 weeks. Check weekly to make sure that the brine level is still above the top of the cabbage. If it isn't, press down on your weight to get the brine to rise back above.

Once you're happy with the acidity, remove the weight, secure the lid, and place the jar in the fridge.

Yield: 1 quart (900 g)

RECIPE NOTE

If you don't want to slice into an eggplant for just four slices, you can absolutely omit it. It does make for a fun, visual addition, however.

Ingredients

- 2 pounds (900 g) cabbage

- 4 teaspoons (22 g) kosher salt

- 2 tablespoons (13 g) caraway seeds

NEW WORLD RYE KRAUT

A local fermentation expert and baker, Alex Bois, makes some astounding breads for a fantastic Philadelphia restaurant called High Street on Market. One of my favorite loaves is a deceptively simple sandwich rye. This sauerkraut is an ode to that bread. When I'm feeling extra adoration for the humble caraway seed, I will toast up a slice of Bois's New World Rye bread, butter it, and top it with a heaping pile of this kraut for breakfast.

Remove any unattractive or wilted outer leaves from the cabbage, reserving one. Cut out the core and rinse the cabbage. Shred the cabbage into ¼-inch (0.5 cm) wide strips. Place in a large bowl, add the salt, and toss thoroughly for about 30 seconds or until the cabbage has a sheen of moisture on it.

Gently massage and squeeze the cabbage until there is a visible puddle of water in the bottom of the bowl and the cabbage pieces stay in a clump when squeezed. Add the caraway seeds and toss to distribute evenly.

Pack the mixture into a clean quart (1 L) jar. First, pack it along the bottom using the top of your fist or your fingers. Continue packing in this fashion, pressing along the sides and bottom, until it comes to 1½ to 2 inches (4 to 5 cm) below the rim. If you need more space, press down on the cabbage and tilt the jar to pour the cabbage liquid back into the bowl.

Use the reserved cabbage leaf to create a "cabbage shelf" (see page 75). Pour the cabbage liquid from the bowl into the jar to cover the cabbage. Leave 1 to 1½ inches (2.5 to 4 cm) of headspace at the top of the jar. Using your preferred method (see pages 23 to 28), weight the cabbage down and cover your jar.

Allow to ferment at room temperature for 3 to 4 weeks. Check weekly to make sure that the brine level is still above the top of the cabbage. If it isn't, press down on the weight to raise the brine level.

Once you're happy with the acidity, remove the weight, secure the lid, and place the jar in the fridge.

Yield: 1 quart (900 g)

Ingredients

- 1 head cabbage (about 2 pounds, or 900 g)
- 1 tablespoon (18 g) kosher salt
- ¼ cup (34 g) unsalted, raw macadamia nuts, coarsely chopped
- ¼ cup (31 g) unsalted, raw pistachios, coarsely chopped
- ¼ cup (35 g) unsalted, raw cashews, coarsely chopped
- ¼ cup (57 g) shelled, raw, unsalted pumpkin seeds

NUTS FOR KRAUT

Some people may think I'm nuts for putting nuts in kraut, but it's an extremely healthful choice. Nuts and seeds contain phytates, which bind to nutrients and prevent them from being absorbed by our bodies. Happily, fermentation eliminates phytic acid, transforming nuts and seeds into health foods, rather than nutrient blockers. The nuts soften during fermentation, while the seeds tend to stay crunchy. Both take on a little sour flavor, which is half the fun! Feel free to substitute whatever nuts and seeds you have.

Remove any unattractive or wilted outer leaves from the cabbage, reserving one. Cut out the core and rinse the cabbage. Shred the cabbage into ¼-inch (0.5 cm) wide strips. Place in a large bowl, add the salt, and toss thoroughly for about 30 seconds or until the cabbage has a sheen of moisture on it.

Massage and squeeze the cabbage until there is a visible puddle of water in the bottom of the bowl and the cabbage pieces stay in a clump when squeezed. Pour all the nuts and the pumpkin seeds into the bowl and toss to distribute evenly.

Pack the mixture into a clean quart (1 L) jar using the top of your fist or your fingers. Continue packing in this fashion, pressing along the sides and bottom, until it comes to 1½ to 2 inches (4 to 5 cm) below the rim. If you need more space, press down on the cabbage and tilt the jar to pour the cabbage liquid back into the bowl.

Use the reserved cabbage leaf to create a "cabbage shelf" (see page 75). Pour the cabbage liquid from the bowl into the jar to cover the cabbage. Leave 1 to 1½ inches (2.5 to 4 cm) of headspace at the top of the jar. Using your preferred method (see pages 23 to 28), weight the cabbage down and cover your jar.

Allow to ferment at room temperature for 2 to 4 weeks, checking at least once a week to make sure that the brine level is still above the top of the cabbage. If it isn't, press down on your weight to get the brine to rise back above.

Once you're happy with the acidity, remove the weight, secure the lid, and place the jar in the fridge.

Yield: 1 quart (900 g)

Ingredients

- 2 pounds (900 g) cabbage
- 2 teaspoons (12 g) kosher salt
- 1 teaspoon (1 g) red pepper flakes
- 2 tablespoons (30 ml) soy sauce
- ½ cup (130 g) creamy peanut butter
- 1 tablespoon (15 ml) toasted sesame oil
- 1 teaspoon (2 g) coriander seeds
- 1 red bell pepper, seeded and chopped
- Fresh cilantro, for serving (optional)

SAUERKRAUT SATAY

I genuinely cannot stop eating cold sesame noodles when I have them in the house, so I developed this recipe as a better-for-me alternative. The flavors in this kraut are just about a perfect match for cold sesame noodles at 5 to 7 days of fermentation, but it still tastes great after a full month of fermentation.

Remove any unattractive or wilted outer leaves from the cabbage, reserving one. Cut out the core and rinse the cabbage.

Grate the cabbage using a box grater or the grating blade on your food processor. Place in a large bowl, add the salt, and toss thoroughly for about 30 seconds or until the cabbage has a sheen of moisture on it.

Gently massage and squeeze the cabbage until there is a visible puddle of water in the bottom of the bowl and the cabbage pieces stay in a clump when squeezed. Add the red pepper flakes, soy sauce, peanut butter, oil, coriander, and bell pepper and toss to distribute.

Pack the mixture into a clean quart (1 L) jar. Pack it along the bottom using the top of your fist or your fingers. Continue packing in this fashion, pressing along the sides and bottom, until it comes to 1½ to 2 inches (4 to 5 cm) below the rim. If you need more space, press down on the cabbage and tilt the jar to pour the cabbage liquid back into the bowl.

Use the reserved cabbage leaf to create a "cabbage shelf" (see page 75). The cabbage shelf is essential in this recipe. If the peanut butter is exposed to air during fermentation its oils can oxidize and turn rancid. Pour the cabbage liquid from the bowl into the jar to cover the cabbage. Leave 1 to 1½ inches (2.5 to 4 cm) of headspace at the top of the jar. Using your preferred method (see pages 23 to 28), weight the cabbage down and cover your jar.

Allow to ferment at room temperature for 5 to 10 days. If you ferment for longer than that, be sure to check that the brine level is above the top of the cabbage. If it isn't, press down on your weight to get the brine to rise back above.

Once you're happy with the acidity, remove the weight, secure the lid, and place the jar in the fridge. Serve sprinkled with cilantro.

Yield: 1 quart (900 g)

Ingredients

1½ pounds (675 g) cabbage

2-inch (5 cm) piece of ginger, unpeeled

4 teaspoons (22 g) kosher salt

1 small beet (½ pound, or 225 g)

GINGER BEET KRAUT

Sometimes simplicity makes for the ultimate crowd-pleaser. In this case, just a couple of ingredients make an unforgettable sauerkraut that complements just about anything you can put on a plate. Try it in pasta or tossed salads for a burst of flavor and color.

Remove any unattractive or wilted outer leaves from the cabbage, reserving one. Cut out the core and rinse the cabbage. Grate the cabbage and ginger using a box grater or the grating blade on your food processor. Place in a large bowl, add the salt, and toss thoroughly until the cabbage has a sheen of moisture on it. Trim and quarter the beets and cut the quarters into ¼-inch (5 mm) thick slices. Add the beets to the cabbage.

Gently massage and squeeze the cabbage until there is a visible puddle in the bottom of the bowl and the cabbage pieces stay in a clump when squeezed.

Pack the mixture into a clean quart (1 L) jar. First, pack it along the bottom using the top of your fist or your fingers. Continue packing in this fashion, pressing along the sides and bottom, until the cabbage comes to 2 inches (5 cm) below the rim. If you need more space, press down on the cabbage and tilt the jar to pour the cabbage liquid back into the bowl.

Use the reserved cabbage leaf to create a "cabbage shelf" (see page 75). Pour the cabbage liquid from the bowl into the jar. Leave at least 1 inch (2.5 cm) of headspace at the top of the jar. Using your preferred method (see pages 23 to 28), weight the veggies down and cover your jar.

Allow to ferment at room temperature for 3 to 4 weeks, checking once a week to make sure that the brine level is still above the top of the cabbage. If it isn't, press down on your weight to get the brine to rise back above.

Once you're happy with the acidity, remove the weight, secure the lid, and place the jar in the fridge.

Yield: 1 quart (900 g)

Extra Cabbage Liquid?

So what do you do with that salty cabbage water that accrues in your bowl during the massage period? Most people just discard it, but it is salty and vegetal, so it makes a great addition to soups, stocks, and even bread-baking liquid. Another option is to store it in a labeled jar in your fridge. If your brine level evaporates, you can just pour it over your cabbage shelf and know that it's the perfect salinity for your kraut.

Ingredients

- 3 cups (675 g) finished sauerkraut, such as Ginger Beet Kraut (page 91)

- 4 hard-boiled eggs, cooled and peeled

SAUERKRAUT PICKLED EGGS

I don't know if this makes me a weirdo, but I go CRAZY for pickled eggs. This technique can also be done in brined ferments, kimchi liquid, and any other vegetable ferment you let go long enough for acidity to get appropriately low. The truly awesome thing about fermented pickled eggs isn't their utterly superior flavor—it's the fun games you can play with color! Use a red kraut to end up with purple eggs, radish pickle brine for pastel pink, or finished beet kvass for a beet red egg.

Put about an inch (2.5 cm) of sauerkraut that has fermented for a minimum of 2 weeks into a quart (1 L) jar. Pack extra around the sides to create a little crater in the jar. Place an egg into the crater and gently pack more sauerkraut on top and fit another egg in. Cover that egg with more sauerkraut and pack the whole thing, very gently, down. Repeat with the remaining 2 eggs, ending with at least a thin layer of sauerkraut on top.

Place the jar in the fridge and allow the eggs to culture and color for 5 days to 2 weeks. You may eat the kraut and eggs as soon as the eggs taste pickled enough for you.

Yield: 4 eggs plus 3 cups (675 g) sauerkraut

You can also put peeled, hard-boiled eggs into finished pickle brines. The resulting pickled eggs are rainbow-colored and delicious. It is okay to put unpeeled eggs, or eggs with intentionally cracked shells, into the mix. The lactic acid will eat away at the shells and provide you with some very interesting patterns and colors. If you do use unpeeled eggs, don't eat the sauerkraut as the alkaline in the shells can result in a higher pH.

Ingredients

- 1¾ pounds (790 g) cabbage
- 4 teaspoons (22 g) kosher salt
- 2 carrots
- ½ small onion, peeled
- 1½ celery stalks
- 1 teaspoon (1.5 g) dried thyme leaves
- 1 teaspoon (1 g) dried sage leaves
- 4 whole, unblemished bay leaves

MIREPOIX KRAUT

The combination of celery, onions, and carrots is such a classic in French cooking that it is often referred to as the "Holy Trinity." In this kraut, the classic flavors of mirepoix and bouquet garni are combined to make a jar that would serve just as well as a centerpiece for a family meal as it would as a side dish. Serve alongside your favorite chicken dishes for a little French flair.

Remove any unattractive or wilted outer leaves from the cabbage, reserving one. Cut out the core and rinse the cabbage. Shred the cabbage into ¼-inch (0.5 cm) wide strips. Place in a large bowl, add the salt, and toss thoroughly for about 30 seconds or until the cabbage has a sheen of moisture on it.

Let the salt and cabbage sit while you dice the carrots, onion, and celery. Gently massage and squeeze the cabbage until there is a visible puddle of water in the bottom of the bowl and the cabbage pieces stay in a clump when squeezed. Add the diced vegetables, thyme, and sage to the cabbage mixture and toss to distribute.

Tightly pack a small amount of the cabbage mixture into the bottom of a quart (1 L) jar. Gently slide the stem end of 1 bay leaf down along the side of the jar, securing part of it in the cabbage mixture so that it is pressed flat against the side of the jar. Pack more cabbage into the jar, gently so that the bay leaf is pressed against the glass but not pushed down and broken. On another side of the jar, place another bay leaf and secure against the glass by pressing more cabbage mixture into the jar. Repeat until there is 1 bay leaf visible on each side of the jar and all of the cabbage mixture is pressed in, to about 1½ to 2 inches (4 to 5 cm) below the rim. If you need more space, press down on the cabbage and tilt the jar to pour the cabbage liquid back into the bowl.

Use the reserved cabbage leaf to create a "cabbage shelf" (see page 75). Pour the cabbage liquid from the bowl into the jar to cover the cabbage. Leave ¾ to 1 inch (2 to 2.5 cm) of headspace at the top of the jar. Using your preferred method (see pages 23 to 28), weight the veggies down and cover your jar.

Allow to ferment at room temperature for 4 to 6 weeks, checking at least once a week to make sure that the brine level is still above the top of the cabbage. If it isn't, press down on your weight to get the brine to rise back above. Once you're happy with the acidity, remove the weight, secure the lid, and place the jar in the fridge.

Yield: 1 quart (900 g)

Ingredients

2 pounds (900 g) cabbage

4 teaspoons (22 g) salt

Zest of 1 lemon

Zest of 1 lime

Zest of ½ of an orange

SUPER SOUR CITRUS KRAUT

Citrus zest is one of the most useful and versatile seasonings in any cook's arsenal. It can go sweet or it can go savory. In this simple kraut, the combination of three citrus zests makes for a punchy, party-worthy kraut. When using citrus peel or zest in any ferment, leave the pith out to avoid unpleasant bitterness.

Remove any unattractive or wilted outer leaves from the cabbage, reserving one. Cut out the core and rinse the cabbage. Shred the cabbage into ¼-inch (0.5 cm) wide strips. Place in a large bowl, add the salt, and toss thoroughly for about 30 seconds or until the cabbage has a sheen of moisture on it.

Gently massage and squeeze the cabbage until there is a visible puddle of water in the bottom of the bowl and the cabbage pieces stay in a clump when squeezed. Add the zests and toss for a minute to evenly distribute.

Pack the mixture into a clean quart (1 L) jar. First, pack it along the bottom using the top of your fist or your fingers. Continue packing in this fashion, pressing along the sides and bottom, until it comes to 1½ to 2 inches (4 to 5 cm) below the rim. If you need more space, press down on the cabbage and tilt the jar to pour the cabbage liquid back into the bowl.

Use the reserved cabbage leaf to create a "cabbage shelf" (see page 75). Pour the cabbage liquid from the bowl into the jar to cover the cabbage. Leave 1 to 1½ inches (2.5 to 4 cm) of headspace at the top of the jar. Using your preferred method (see pages 23 to 28), weight the cabbage down and cover your jar.

Place your jar on a small plate or bowl and allow to ferment at room temperature for 3 to 4 weeks. Check weekly to make sure that the brine level is still above the top of the cabbage. If it isn't, press down on your weight to get the brine to rise back above. Once you're happy with the acidity, remove the weight, secure the lid, and place the jar in the fridge.

Yield: 1 quart (900 g)

Ingredients

- 2 pounds (900 g) cabbage
- 2 tablespoons (36 g) kosher salt
- 1 tablespoon (11 g) mustard seed
- 4 inches (10 cm) of fresh ginger, unpeeled
- 4 organic, thin-skinned, unwaxed lemons

PRESERVED LEMON GINGER KRAUT

One of the best parts about this kraut is that when it's done, you have kraut *and* preserved lemon slices. Eat them in your kraut or chop them up, peel and all, and throw them in just about anything from salads to grain dishes for an amazing flavor boost. I make this kraut for fermentation events and it's always a crowd-pleaser.

Remove any unattractive or wilted outer leaves from the cabbage, reserving one. Cut out the core and rinse the cabbage. Shred the cabbage into ¼-inch (0.5 cm) wide strips. Place in a large bowl, add the salt, and toss thoroughly for about 30 seconds or until the cabbage has a sheen of moisture on it. Mix in the mustard seed and set aside.

Grate the ginger and add to the cabbage bowl. Remove the ends from your lemons and then slice them very thinly.

Massage the cabbage mixture well until there is a puddle in the bottom of the bowl and the cabbage stays together in a clump when squeezed.

Place a large handful of cabbage into a quart (1 L) jar and pack it in tightly. Layer slices from 1 lemon evenly over the cabbage in the jar. Pack more cabbage mixture on top of the lemon slices and repeat these layers until the ingredients are all in the jar, ending with a cabbage layer packed 2 inches (5 cm) below the rim of the jar.

Use the reserved cabbage leaf to create a "cabbage shelf" (see page 75). Pour the cabbage liquid from the bowl into the jar to cover the cabbage. Leave 1 inch (2.5 cm) of headspace at the top of the jar. Using your preferred method (see pages 23 to 28), weight the cabbage down and cover your jar.

Allow to ferment at room temperature for 4 to 8 weeks, checking weekly to make sure that the brine is still covering the cabbage. If it isn't, press down on the weight to raise the brine level.

Once you're happy with the acidity, remove the weight, secure the lid, and place the jar in the fridge.

Yield: 1 quart (900 g)

Ingredients

- 1¾ pounds (790 g) cabbage
- 2 carrots
- 1 tablespoon (18 g) kosher salt
- 1 inch (2.5 cm) piece of ginger, unpeeled and grated
- 1 teaspoon (2.5 g) ground cinnamon
- ½ teaspoon (1 g) ground nutmeg
- ½ cup (55 g) pecans, coarsely chopped
- ¼ cup (35 g) unsweetened raisins

CARROT CAKE KRAUT

A few years ago, I started referring to some of my krauts as "dessert krauts." Some find that funny until, that is, they devour the kraut in question. The concept of dessert kraut may not be fully intuitive, but somehow, it works. Abandon sugar cravings, all ye who make this kraut.

Remove any unattractive or wilted outer leaves from the cabbage, reserving one. Cut out the core. Shred the cabbage into ¼-inch (0.5 cm) wide strips and grate the carrots. Place both in a large bowl, add salt, and toss and squeeze until the cabbage has a sheen of moisture on it.

Gently massage and squeeze the cabbage, or let it sit for a bit, to make the work easier, until there is a visible puddle of water in the bottom of the bowl.

Add the ginger, cinnamon, nutmeg, pecans, and raisins and continue to massage, mixing them in as you go, until the cabbage pieces stay in a clump when squeezed.

Press the mixture into a clean quart (1 L) jar using the top of your fist and your fingers to pack it along the sides and bottom. Stop packing when the jar is full to 2 inches (5 cm) below the rim. If you need more space, press down on the cabbage in the jar and tilt the jar to pour the cabbage liquid back into the bowl.

Use the reserved cabbage leaf to create a "cabbage shelf" (see page 75). Pour the liquid from the bowl into the jar to cover the cabbage. Leave at least 1 inch (2.5 cm) of headspace at the top of the jar. Using your preferred method (see pages 23 to 28), weight the veggies down and cover your jar.

Allow to ferment at room temperature for 2 to 4 weeks. Check weekly to make sure that the brine is still covering the cabbage. If it isn't, press down on the weight to raise the brine level.

Once you're happy with the acidity, remove the weight, secure the lid, and place the jar in the fridge.

Yield: 1 quart (900 g)

CHAPTER THREE

Kimchi

 Kimchi is one of the world's best-known fermented foods and is *the* most culturally important food of Korea, even boasting its own museum in Seoul.

There is no limit to where you can find kimchi popping up in traditional and nontraditional kitchens alike; in Korea—and, increasingly, abroad—kimchi is commonly eaten at every meal. Have kimchi with eggs just one morning for breakfast and there's a good chance you'll be hooked.

While we in the West tend to think of kimchi as spicy, salty, delightfully pungent napa cabbage, kimchi is actually many things. There are well over 100 "official" versions of kimchi, and that number doesn't include home-made versions that cater to the taste preferences of specific families. In this chapter, we'll explore both traditional and decidedly nontraditional styles. I know from my readers that families often have their preferred version, made special by that secret ingredient no one else uses. Perhaps through experimentation, you'll make your family a kimchi classic to be handed down through the generations.

Kimchi Considerations

Following are a few elements of kimchi for you to consider before getting your ferments rolling.

Chopping

There are forms of kimchi that are named specifically for the way the vegetables used in it are chopped (Nabak Kimchi, page 121). The size of the pieces will also impact fermentation time; larger pieces will take longer to reach the same acidity as smaller ones.

Salting

The decision to salt or brine is a personal one. Salting (applying a large amount directly to your cabbage) takes less time but uses much more salt. The cabbage is rinsed after salting to remove excess salt, so what goes into your final product doesn't taste a lot saltier than a brined batch.
In brining (creating a brine of water and salt and then submerging your cabbage and daikon in it), you'll use a much smaller quantity of salt, but you'll need to let it sit for a minimum of 12 hours before you start actually composing your kimchi. The choice is yours. The final result is very similar.

Timing

How long you ferment your kimchi depends on several factors: the vegetables used, the time of year, temperature, and, most importantly, taste preferences. I adore the flavors of lightly fermented and even unfermented kimchi, and I often ferment it for only 3 to 7 days. But after weeks or months of fermentation, it will be something totally different. Some friends won't even consider eating it until it is soft and fizzy, which can take months of fermentation depending on the temperature and sugar and salt levels. If you're making it for long aging, use a bit more salt than is found in these recipes.

Kimchi Gloves

Many of the ingredients that make kimchi taste so amazing can irritate your skin (hot pepper and ginger) or make your hands smell a bit too delicious (fish sauce, garlic, or onion). Elegant Korean women have special pink rubber gloves for the express purpose of mixing kimchi. If you have a Korean market in your area, you will be able to find these; otherwise, feel free to use disposable latex gloves or rubber dishwashing gloves, reserved for fermenting, to protect your hands and keep them from smelling like garlic and fish sauce for a week!

Common Kimchi Ingredients

- **Napa cabbage.** Napa cabbage is white, green, and capsule-shaped and has a wider and softer rib than those from the hard, round heads of green cabbage more commonly found in American grocery stores. Look for a head that is heavy for its size. Lighter large heads, especially out of season, sometimes look nice on the outside but have brown, wilting leaves on the inside.
- **Daikon**. Daikon is actually the Japanese name for the long, white, relatively mild radish that is found in so many kinds of kimchi. The very similar Korean version, mu, is rounder and shorter and has a greener top, but daikon is usually easier to find in American markets.
- **Korean red pepper powder (Gochugaru).** You can find gochugaru (Korean red pepper powder) in either a coarse or a fine grind. The coarse version was used in these recipes. In spite of kimchi's reputation as a very spicy food, gochugaru isn't all that hot. If you want to amp up the heat, add red pepper flakes or even fresh hot peppers in the blending stage. Be aware that adding fresh peppers will alter the color of your red kimchi, often resulting in an orangish hue after a few days of fermentation.
- **Fish sauce**. The fish sauce you include in your kimchi will provide an enormous amount of umami flavor and, frankly, an enormous amount of aroma during fermentation. Choose a fish sauce that has only two ingredients: anchovies and salt. Vegans and vegetarians should feel free to omit fish sauce and salted shrimp from all recipes.
- **Salted shrimp (saewoo juht)**. These little guys, found at just about any Asian grocery store, come in refrigerated jars, packed in liquid. They should be drained before using.
- **Korean chives**. Korean chives look like large, flat blades of grass and have a mild onion flavor. Their larger cousins, Chinese chives, are available at any Asian market and they make a great substitute for the Korean version. If you can't find either, scallions are a suitable replacement.
- **Rice flour**. Rice flour can be found at most markets. Look for finely ground rice flour. If you have trouble finding it, you can omit it entirely or substitute puréed fruit, all-purpose flour, or another starchy flour (nut and coconut flours are not recommended).
- **Ginger**. Fresh ginger is an essential element to the flavor of kimchi. It is ususally blended in, so no laborious peeling of its papery skin is necessary.
- **Sugar**. As with any iconic food, taste preferences for kimchi vary wildly. If you're the type who likes a soft and fizzy kimchi, add 1 to 2 teaspoons (4 to 8 g) of sugar per quart (1 L) of kimchi before fermentation and another 1 teaspoon (4 g) to the jar just before refrigeration. I don't use sugar in my home kimchi, so these recipes do not call for added sugar, but know that it is a commonly used ingredient.

EVERYDAY BAECHU KIMCHI

Baechu is the Korean word for one of the most common kimchi ingredients, napa cabbage. Baechu kimchi is the kimchi that we most often see in Korean restaurants in the United States. It's red. It's spicy. It's seductive. This is the kimchi I make most frequently, often in large batches to avoid the outrage that occurs when we run out. There is no end to the uses for this kimchi. We use it in Mac and Kimcheese (page 116) and as an ingredient in just about every omelet or batch of scrambled eggs I make. If I'm being totally honest, though, we most commonly eat this kimchi straight from the jar.

Ingredients

- One 2-pound (900 g) head napa cabbage
- 5 tablespoons (100 g) kosher salt
- 8¾ cups (2 L) filtered water, divided
- 1½ tablespoons (15 g) rice flour
- ½ pound (225 g) daikon
- 1 inch (2.5 cm) of ginger
- ½ small onion, peeled
- 4 cloves of garlic, peeled
- 1 tablespoon (4 g) red pepper flakes
- ½ cup (60 g) coarse grind gochugaru
- 1 tablespoon (15 ml) fish sauce
- 1 tablespoon (8 g) drained, salted shrimp
- 5 stems of Chinese chives, 8 to 9 stems Korean chives, or 5 scallions

Soak the napa cabbage or rinse thoroughly in cool water to remove any dirt or debris trapped within its leaves. Rinse the cabbage head and pat dry. Halve the cabbage and remove the core. Slice each half into quarters. You will now have 8 long strips of napa cabbage. If the strips are wider than 2 inches (5 cm), halve them again lengthwise. Cut horizontally across each strip to create 1- to 2-inch (2.5 to 5 cm) chunks. The chunks will separate into individual pieces as they're chopped. Place all the cabbage pieces into a large bowl.

Pour the salt into 8 cups (1.9 L) of the water and stir to dissolve. Pour the mixture over the cabbage in the bowl. Use a plate or another food-safe, nonmetallic item to keep the vegetables submerged under the brine. Allow to soak for 12 to 24 hours.

After soaking, thoroughly drain the cabbage and pat dry.

In your smallest saucepan, bring the remaining ¾ cup (175 ml) water and the rice flour to a boil over medium-high heat, whisking constantly. Reduce the heat to medium and continue whisking until the mixture thickens, about 2 minutes. Transfer the paste to a clean bowl and refrigerate to chill and thicken further.

While the rice paste is cooling, remove the crown and greens from the daikon and reserve for another use. Cut the daikon into ¼- to ½-inch (5 mm to 1.5 cm) sticks and toss the daikon and cabbage together in a large bowl.

Coarsely chop the unpeeled ginger, onion, and garlic and place in the bowl of a food processor along with the red pepper flakes, gochugaru, fish sauce, shrimp, and cooled rice paste. Blend until it becomes a smooth paste, scraping down the sides of the bowl as necessary. Chop the chives into 2-inch (5 cm) pieces. Add to the bowl with the cabbage and daikon.

Put on your kimchi gloves, if desired. Scoop the blended rice paste into the bowl with the vegetables and use your hands to mix the ingredients together and to coat the vegetables. Once the ingredients are well mixed, remove the glove from your nondominant hand and use that hand to hold a clean quart (1 L) jar.

Pack the mixture in the bowl tightly into the jar, leaving an inch (2.5 cm) of head-space at the top of the jar. Wipe the rim of the jar with a clean, damp cloth to remove any paste that may have clung there. Using your preferred method (see pages 23 to 28), weight the kimchi down and cover your jar. You may also choose not to use a weight for this recipe, since kimchi is not prone to surface issues.

Allow to ferment at room temperature for 3 to 7 days. Remove the weight, secure the lid, and place the jar in the fridge.

Yield: 1 quart (900 g)

Ingredients

- 2 tablespoons (30 ml) olive oil
- 1 onion, sliced
- 1 small head of cauliflower, cut into small florets
- 2 small apples, cored and coarsely chopped
- 1 cup (235 ml) kimchi liquid

KIMCHI-BRAISED CAULIFLOWER AND APPLES

To the likely dismay of my overcrowded refrigerator, I have a very hard time dumping the liquids left over from my vegetable ferments. Kimchi liquid, in particular, packs a ton of flavor, and I find it hard to toss. Does that make me a hoarder? Nah. The brines and juices of my fermented vegetables never hang around long. We eat them up! To get liquid from kimchi, either strain the kimchi through mesh strainers or wait until you've eaten the vegetables and reserve what's left.

Heat the oil in a heavy-bottomed saucepan or Dutch or French oven and add the onion. Cook over medium heat until soft but not browned, about 5 minutes.

Add the cauliflower and apples and stir to coat in the oil. Continue cooking, stirring occasionally, until both have softened, about 10 minutes. Add the kimchi liquid and lower the heat. Cover and allow to simmer for 15 to 20 minutes or until all of the kimchi liquid has been absorbed. Serve hot.

Yield: 6 cups (1.4 kg)

Scaling Up the Rice Paste

Many kimchi recipes call for rice paste. If you're making a larger batch than called for here or if you are planning on making several recipes within a few days, making a larger batch of the paste and storing it in the fridge makes sense. Use 2 tablespoons (20 g) of rice flour per cup (235 ml) of water and know that larger batches take longer to boil and thicken. Larger batches will also experience less evaporation, so plan to use anywhere from ¼ to ½ cup (60 to 120 g) finished rice paste in these kimchi recipes.

If brining your vegetables, it makes sense to make the rice paste when you start the brining. Just store it in the fridge until you're ready to use it. (You can store the finished paste in the fridge for up to 3 days before it starts to break down.)

Ingredients

- 1½ pounds (680 g) napa cabbage
- 1 medium daikon (8 ounces, or 225 g)
- 4 tablespoons (80 g) kosher salt
- 9 cups (2.1 L) filtered water, divided
- 2 tablespoons (20 g) rice flour
- Two 4-inch (10 cm) pieces of fresh lemongrass core
- 4 inches (10 cm) of ginger
- 8 cloves of garlic, peeled
- 4 or 5 Thai (bird's-eye) chiles or habaneros
- ½ small onion
- 2 tablespoons (30 ml) fish sauce
- 1 tablespoon (4 g) red pepper flakes
- 5 scallions
- 6 fresh or frozen kaffir lime leaves

THAI-CHI

This playful and spicy kimchi incorporates some of my favorite ingredients from the Thai take-out menu. Kaffir lime leaves make a great addition to soups and stocks and they flavor beverages beautifully, but they can be omitted or imperfectly replaced by a teaspoon (2 g) of fresh lime zest.

Soak the napa cabbage thoroughly to remove any debris and dirt. Halve it and remove the core. Slice each half into quarters. You will now have 8 long strips of napa cabbage. Cut horizontally across each strip to create 1- to 2-inch (2.5 to 5 cm) chunks. The chunks will separate into pieces as they're chopped. Place all the cabbage pieces into a very large bowl.

Remove the crown and greens from the daikon and reserve for another use. Cut it into ¼-inch (5 mm) wide, 2-inch (5 cm) long strips and add to the bowl with the cabbage.

Pour the salt into 8 cups (1.9 L) of the water and stir to dissolve. Pour the mixture over the cabbage and daikon in the bowl. Use a plate to keep the vegetables submerged under the brine. Allow to soak for 12 to 24 hours.

After soaking, bring the remaining 1 cup (235 ml) water and the rice flour to a boil in your smallest saucepan, whisking constantly. Reduce the heat to medium and continue whisking until the mixture thickens, about 2 minutes. Transfer the paste to a clean bowl and refrigerate to chill and thicken further.

Cut the lemongrass into thin rounds and the scallions into 2-inch (5 cm) pieces.

Put the cooled flour mixture, ginger, garlic, chiles, onion, fish sauce, and red pepper flakes into a food processor and blend until mostly smooth. Toss the scallions, lemongrass, lime leaves, and chile/onion mixture with vegetables until they are well coated and the scallions, lemongrass and lime leaves are distributed throughout the mixture. Pack very tightly into a quart (1 L) jar and cover loosely with a lid.

Allow to ferment at room temperature from 1 to 3 weeks. Once you're happy with the flavor, secure the jar lid and store in the fridge.

Yield: 1 quart (900 g)

Ingredients

½ large head of napa cabbage (2 pounds, or 900 g)

½ cup (145 g) kosher salt

9 cups (2.1 L) filtered water, divided

2 tablespoons (20 g) rice flour

½ pound (225 g) daikon

½ bunch of Korean chives

3 inches (7.5 cm) of ginger, unpeeled

¼ small onion

4 cloves of garlic, peeled

1 tablespoon (15 ml) fish sauce

¾ cup (90 g) gochugaru

HALF HEAD KIMCHI

Not only is this kimchi fun to make, but it's also the perfect company kimchi. It serves as a centerpiece until dinnertime (see photo on page 100), when I ceremoniously carve it like a Thanksgiving turkey. Each guest gets a 2- to 3-inch (5 to 7.5 cm) thick cross-section to devour. If we're not expecting company, I often peel leaves off one by one and use them as incredibly flavorful (and messy) wraps for whatever I'm having for lunch.

Soak the napa cabbage or rinse thoroughly in cool water to remove any dirt or debris trapped within its leaves and halve it lengthwise. Either make two batches or use the other half of the cabbage for another purpose.

Add the salt to 8 cups (1.9 L) of the water and stir to dissolve. Place the cabbage in a large bowl and pour the salt water over it. Use a plate or another food-safe, nonmetallic item to keep it submerged under the brine. Allow to soak for 24 hours.

After brining, thoroughly drain and rinse all sides of the cabbage in cool water, being careful to support the head so that it does not break apart.

In a small saucepan, bring the flour and remaining 1 cup (235 ml) water to a boil over medium-high heat, whisking constantly. Reduce the heat to medium and continue whisking until the mixture thickens, about 4 minutes. Transfer the paste to a clean bowl and refrigerate to chill and thicken further.

While the rice paste is cooling, remove the crown and greens from the daikon and reserve for another use. Cut the daikon into small matchsticks with a maximum width of ¼ inch (5 mm). The mandoline comes in handy for this task. Place in a bowl.

Chop the chives into 2-inch (5 cm) pieces and add them to the bowl with the daikon.

Coarsely chop the unpeeled ginger, onion, and garlic and place into the bowl of a food processor along with the fish sauce, gochugaru, and cooled flour mixture. Blend into a smooth paste, scraping down the sides as necessary.

Put on your kimchi gloves. Scoop the blended rice paste into the bowl with the vegetables and use your hands to mix the ingredients together and to coat the vegetables.

Hold the half cabbage in your nondominant hand or place it on a clean plate, cut-side up. Working from the smallest, center leaves outward, rub handfuls of rice paste mixture in between each leaf. Be gentle and careful not to pull the leaves out. Each leaf should be fully coated inside and out with the mix. Once you've rubbed the mixture between each leaf, rub most of the remaining paste over all the outer surfaces of the cabbage.

Carefully place the cabbage into your fermenting container. Keep as many vegetables as possible inside. Rub any remaining paste over the exposed surface of the cabbage. Place a lid on the container and wipe the sides and lid with a clean, wet cloth.

Place the container on a plate and ferment for 7 to 10 days at room temperature. Once you're happy with the flavor, move it to the refrigerator until an hour before serving. To serve, carefully remove the cabbage from the container, again being careful not to lose too much of the mixture packed between the leaves, and place cut-side down on a small serving platter.

Yield: 5 to 6 servings

RECIPE NOTE You will need to find a tight-fitting container in which to ferment this kimchi. I find that a glass loaf pan with a tight-fitting lid works well for a head this size. Try various sizes to see what fits best for you.

Ingredients

- 1 head (2 pounds, or 900 g) red cabbage
- 6 tablespoons (110 g) kosher salt
- 9 cups (2.1 L) filtered water, divided
- 2½ tablespoons (25 g) all-purpose flour
- 4 or 5 cherry bell or French breakfast radishes (4 ounces, or 115 g), greens and roots removed
- 5 scallions
- 1 red bell pepper (7 ounces, or 200 g)
- 2 small, fresh red hot peppers
- 2 cloves of garlic, peeled
- 1 small onion, peeled
- 1½ teaspoons (2 g) red pepper flakes
- 1½ teaspoons (3 g) cayenne pepper
- 1 teaspoon (2 g) ground ginger
- 1 teaspoon (5 ml) soy sauce

AMERICAN SEOUL KIMCHI

This kimchi creation was made with ingredients that are easily found in American grocery stores. The flavor and texture are miles away from the traditional baechu kimchi (page 104), but it sure is a nice spicy alternative for those without access to specialty Korean ingredients. This is proof that although using the ingredients you have access to might not give you "the real thing," it can often result in something special.

Cut the cabbage in half, cut out the core, and then cut each half into quarters. Cut each resulting wedge crosswise into 4 squarish pieces. Cut longer, rectangular pieces in half to make cubes.

Place the cabbage in a large bowl. Dissolve the salt in 8 cups (1.9 L) of the filtered water and pour the mixture over the cabbage. Keep the cabbage submerged in the brine by placing a weight, such as a small plate, on top and cover the whole thing with a kitchen towel or plastic wrap. Let soak for 12 to 24 hours.

Place the flour and remaining 1 cup (235 ml) water in a small saucepan and turn the heat to high. Stir constantly until boiling and then reduce the heat to medium and continue stirring until the paste has thickened, about 3 to 4 minutes. Transfer to a small bowl and stick it in the fridge to cool completely before using. The mixture will thicken further while cooling, and it may become a tad gummy.

While the rice paste is cooling, strain the cabbage. Slice the radishes into 3 or 4 slices and then cut each slice into 3 or 4 small strips. Trim the scallions and cut them into 1- to 2-inch (2.5 to 5 cm) pieces. Quarter the bell pepper and remove the stem, seeds, and soft inner pith. Remove the crowns and stems from the hot peppers.

Place the cooled flour paste, bell pepper, fresh hot peppers, garlic, onion, red pepper flakes, cayenne, ground ginger, and soy sauce into the bowl of your food processor. Blend until a relatively smooth paste forms, scraping down the sides of the bowl as necessary.

Place the cabbage, radishes, and scallions in a large bowl. Put on your kimchi gloves. Scoop the blended rice paste into the bowl with the vegetables and use your hands to mix the ingredients together and to coat the vegetables.

Pack tightly into two 1-quart (1 L) jars or one ½-gallon (2 L) jar. Wipe the rim of the jar with a clean, damp cloth to remove any paste that may have clung there. Screw the jar lids partially on and place in a room temperature spot away from direct sunlight to ferment for 2 to 6 weeks. Once you're happy with the flavor, tighten the jar lids and store in the fridge.

Yield: 2 quarts (1.8 kg)

Ingredients

- ½ cup (120 ml) filtered water
- 1 tablespoon (10 g) rice flour
- 20 large purple shiso leaves, with at least ½ inch (1.5 cm) of stem, rinsed and patted dry
- Pinch of salt
- 1 clove of garlic, peeled
- ½ inch (1.5 cm) of ginger
- ¼ teaspoon toasted sesame oil
- 1 teaspoon (10 ml) fish sauce
- 1 teaspoon (3 g) coarse grind gochugaru
- 1 teaspoon (3 g) sesame seeds

SHISO LEAF KIMCHI

The Korean concept of *ssam* (wrapping bits of food in a variety of leaves) may just be the original lettuce wrap, and it is definitely my favorite way to eat with my hands. Shiso leaves are on the small side, which makes them perfect for picking up just a bite or two of food. It works great with rice dishes, grilled meats, and *banchan* (small dishes) of all kinds. If you want to be really meta, you can even eat pieces of Pumpkin Spice Kimchi (page 115) in Shiso Leaf Kimchi wraps. The best part of this particular dish is that you're almost required to lick your fingers clean once you're done eating.

In your smallest saucepan, bring the water and rice flour to a boil, whisking constantly. Reduce the heat to medium and continue whisking until the mixture thickens, about 1 minute. Transfer to a bowl and move to the fridge to cool and thicken further.

Once the rice mixture is cool, put it into a blender or food processor along with the salt, garlic, ginger, sesame oil, fish sauce, and gochugaru and blend until smooth. This is a small amount of paste, so you may need to scrape down the sides a few times to get it all mixed in. Stir in the sesame seeds.

Using a small basting brush or gloved fingers, cover the leaves in rice paste. On a small plate, paint a very thin layer over the underside of the largest leaf, from edge to edge, and then flip it over and do the same on the other side. Place the next leaf on top of the painted leaf, bottom side down, and spread paste over it in the same fashion, covering everything but the stem in a thin layer. The rice mix will make the leaves hold together. Continue this process until the leaves are all stacked and covered in paste.

If there is a small amount of rice paste mixture remaining, slather it onto the whole stack. Pick the stack up by the stems and place flat inside a plastic zipper-sealing bag. Press the bag to remove air bubbles and seal. Let it sit for 48 hours in the fridge.

These don't keep long. Enjoy within 24 hours.

Yield: 20 leaves, 2 or 3 servings

Ingredients

½ head (1 pound, or 450 g) napa cabbage

½ small leek

1 small daikon (½ pound, or 225 g)

1 carrot

¼ cup (75 g) kosher salt

8¾ cups (2.1 L) filtered water, divided

4 teaspoons (13 g) rice flour

½ bunch of Korean chives

¼ red or orange bell pepper

3 inches (7.5 cm) of ginger, unpeeled

½ medium onion

2 cloves of garlic, peeled

½ cup (60 g) gochugaru

Two ¼-inch (5 mm) wide pieces of kombu

VERY VEGETABLE VEGAN KIMCHI

I have many vegan friends who love kimchi, so I often make my Everyday Baechu Kimchi (page 104) without fish sauce or salted shrimp so that everyone can enjoy it. This kimchi is a version especially for vegans, with no animal products and a vegetable double down.

Soak the napa cabbage or rinse thoroughly in cool water to remove any dirt or debris trapped within its leaves. Set aside a large leaf for when it's time to pack your jar. Slice each half into quarters. You will now have 8 long strips of napa cabbage. If the strips are wider than 2 inches (5 cm), halve them again lengthwise. Cut horizontally across each strip to create 1- to 2-inch (2.5 to 5 cm) chunks. Place all the cabbage pieces into a large bowl.

Trim the leek and slice it into thin rounds. Soak or rinse well to remove any grit. Remove the crown and greens from the daikon. Remove any roots and cut into ½-inch (1.5 cm) sticks. Trim and coarsely chop the carrot. Add the leek, daikon, and carrot to the bowl of cabbage.

Combine the salt and 8 cups (1.9 L) of the water and stir to dissolve. Pour the mixture over the vegetables in the bowl. Use a plate or another food-safe, nonmetallic item to keep the vegetables submerged under the brine. Soak for at least 12 and up to 24 hours at room temperature. After soaking, drain the vegetables, patting them dry with a clean kitchen towel to get them as dry as possible. Rinse and dry the large brining bowl and then return the vegetables to it.

In a small saucepan, combine the remaining ¾ cup (175 ml) filtered water and rice flour and bring to a boil over medium-high, whisking constantly. Reduce the heat to medium and continue whisking until the mixture thickens, about 2 minutes. Remove from the heat and set aside to cool to room temperature and thicken further.

While the rice paste is cooling, chop the chives into 2-inch (5 cm) long pieces and coarsely chop the bell pepper. Add to the bowl with the drained vegetables.

Coarsely chop the unpeeled ginger, onion, and garlic and place into the bowl of a food processor along with the gochugaru and cooled flour mixture. Blend into a smooth paste, scraping down the sides as necessary.

Put on your kimchi gloves. Scoop the blended rice paste into the bowl with the vegetables, add the kombu, and use your hands to mix the ingredients together and to coat the vegetables in paste. Once the ingredients are well mixed, remove the glove from your nondominant hand and use that hand to hold a clean quart (1 L) jar.

Pack the mixture in the bowl tightly into the jar, leaving 1 to 2 inches (2.5 to 5 cm) of headspace at the top of the jar. Wipe the rim of the jar with a clean, damp cloth to remove any paste that may have clung there. Using your preferred method (see pages 23 to 28), weight the kimchi down and cover your jar. You may also choose not to use a weight for this recipe, since kimchi is not prone to surface issues.

Allow to ferment at room temperature for 3 to 7 days. Once you're happy with the flavor, remove the weight, secure the lid, and place the jar in the fridge.

Yield: 1 quart (900 g)

 RECIPE NOTE If you don't have kombu, you can omit it, or instead, add ¼ teaspoon vegetable bouillon paste into the rice mixture in the blending stage.

Ingredients

- 1 small pumpkin (3 pounds, or 1.4 kg)
- 3 tablespoons (54 g) kosher salt
- 5¾ cups (1.4 L) filtered water, divided
- 4 teaspoons (13 g) rice flour
- ½ small leek (2 ounces, or 60 g), green tops removed
- 4 medium collard leaves
- 3 cloves of garlic, peeled
- 2 inches (5 cm) of ginger
- ¼ cup (30 g) coarse grind gochugaru
- 1 tablespoon (4 g) red pepper flakes
- ½ teaspoon fish sauce
- ½ small onion, coarsely chopped
- 1 small carrot, unpeeled and coarsely chopped
- 1 large cabbage leaf

PUMPKIN SPICE KIMCHI

Whenever the annual pumpkin spice latte freak-out begins, I get excited. I couldn't care less about the latte, but I know it means that I'll soon be able to get my hands on locally grown pumpkins that I can use to make this kimchi. If you can't find small pumpkins, you can substitute just about any winter squash. Kabocha and butternut squash both make fantastic versions of this kimchi.

Cut the pumpkin in half and use a spoon to scoop out and discard the seeds. Cut out the stem and carefully peel the pumpkin. Reserve a few larger strips of pumpkin peel. Slice the peeled pumpkin halves into roughly ½-inch (1.5 cm) cubes. A pointy corner or rounded side here or there is fine.

Place the pumpkin cubes in a bowl. Stir the salt into 5 cups (1.2 L) of the water until dissolved and pour over the pumpkin. Use a small plate or other food-safe, nonmetallic weight to submerge the pumpkin pieces in the brine. Allow to soak for 12 to 24 hours. After brining, drain, pat dry, and place in a large bowl.

In your smallest saucepan, bring the remaining ¾ cup (175 ml) water and the rice flour to a boil over medium-high heat, whisking constantly. Reduce the heat to medium and continue whisking until the mixture thickens, about 2 minutes. Remove from the heat and set aside to cool to room temperature and thicken further.

While the rice paste is cooling, trim the leek and slice it into ⅛-inch (3 mm) or thinner rings. Place the rings in a small bowl and cover with water. Set aside. Remove the stems from the collards and lay the leaves on top of each other. Roll them up and cut into ½-inch (1.5 cm) strips. Place the strips in the bowl with the pumpkin.

Once the rice paste is cool, place it in the bowl of your food processor along with the garlic, ginger, gochugaru, red pepper flakes, fish sauce, onion, and carrot. Process until the mixture is relatively smooth.

Remove the leek from the soaking liquid, being careful not to disturb any grit at the bottom of the bowl, and place it in the bowl with the pumpkin and collard pieces.

Put on your kimchi gloves. Scoop the blended rice paste into the bowl with the vegetables and use your hands to mix the ingredients together and to coat the vegetables. Once the ingredients are well mixed, remove the glove from your nondominant hand and use that hand to hold a clean quart (1 L) jar.

Pack the mixture in the bowl tightly into the jar, leaving an inch (2.5 cm) of headspace at the top of the jar. Wipe the rim of the jar with a clean, damp cloth to remove any paste that may have clung there. Using your preferred method (see pages 23 to 28), weight the kimchi down to submerge it under a thin layer of paste and cover your jar. You may also choose not to use a weight for this recipe, since kimchi is not prone to surface issues.

Ferment at room temperature for 6 days to 3 weeks. Remove the weight, secure the lid, and place the jar in the fridge.

Yield: 1 quart (900 g)

Ingredients

- 8 ounces (225) dried penne pasta
- 1 cup (115 g) shredded Gruyère cheese
- 1 cup (115 g) shredded Cheddar cheese
- 2 tablespoons (16 g) cornstarch
- A few grinds of black pepper
- 1¾ cups (410 ml) whole milk
- 1 teaspoon (4 g) mustard
- 2 tablespoons (28 g) butter
- ½ cup (120 ml) liquid drained from Everyday Baechu or Crock Kimchi (page 104 or 170)
- ¼ cup (75 g) finely chopped Everyday Baechu (page 104) or Radish Kimchi (page 119), plus a bit for garnish

MAC AND KIMCHEESE

Most of the fermented vegetables we eat in our house are consumed raw, sometimes alone, sometimes as sides or mixed into salads. This is the opposite of that. It's pure decadence and it's all about flavor. Serve this at a feast with friends who like to eat and don't expect leftovers. For a larger crowd, double the recipe and bake for an extra 20 to 25 minutes.

Preheat the oven to 375°F (190°C, or gas mark 5).

In a saucepan over medium-high heat, cook the pasta for 5 minutes, drain, and set aside. In a separate bowl, mix the shredded cheeses together and set aside.

In a large saucepan, whisk together the cornstarch, pepper, milk, and mustard. Add the butter and place over medium-high heat. Bring to a boil, stirring constantly, and add the kimchi liquid. Continue to stir until the mixture returns to a boil and then allow it to boil for 1 minute. Remove from the heat and add 1½ cups (175 g) of the cheese and the chopped kimchi. Stir until the cheese is melted and then mix in the pasta.

Pour into a 2-quart (2 L) baking dish and sprinkle with the remaining ½ cup (55 g) cheese. Bake, uncovered, for 25 minutes. Place under the broiler on high for 3 minutes until bubbling and lightly browned. Allow to cool for 10 minutes before eating.

Yield: 4 servings

RECIPE NOTES

- For a gluten-free version, substitute brown rice pasta. Cook the pasta for half the time called for on the package.

- This can be made from start to finish in a Dutch or French oven.

Ingredients

- 1 English cucumber, ends trimmed
- 2½ tablespoons (45 g) kosher salt
- 1 cup (235 ml) filtered water
- 2 tablespoons (20 g) rice flour
- 1 small carrot (2 ounces, or 60 g)
- ½ bunch of Korean chives
- 1 inch (2.5 cm) of ginger, unpeeled
- ¼ cup (30 g) coarse grind gochugaru
- 3 cloves of garlic, peeled

CUCUMBER KIMCHI

There is a traditional stuffed cucumber kimchi (*oi sobagi*) that I love to make. The little stuffed rounds are as beautiful as they are delicious. That version is traditionally not fermented, and it's served as soon as it's made. This fermented adaptation is less beautiful, but the added flavors of fermentation are well worth the visual shift.

Slice the cucumber into 1-inch (2.5 cm) tall rounds. Place the salt in a small bowl and dip each cut side of the cucumber pieces into the salt, coating them entirely in salt. Rub any residual salt over the sides of the cucumber pieces. Place the pieces in a colander in the sink or over a bowl and let them sit overnight to drain. When they've drained for at least 8 hours, rinse them thoroughly in cool water and place in a bowl.

In your smallest saucepan, bring the water and rice flour to a boil, whisking constantly. Reduce the heat to medium and continue whisking until the mixture thickens, 2 to 3 minutes. Remove from the heat and set aside to cool to room temperature.

While the rice paste is cooling, julienne the carrot and cut the chives into 1- to 2-inch (2.5 to 5 cm) pieces. Add to the bowl with the cucumber.

Place the ginger, gochugaru, garlic, and cooled rice paste into the bowl of a food processor and blend until smooth.

Put on your kimchi gloves. Scoop the blended rice paste into the bowl with the vegetables and use your hands to mix the ingredients together and to coat the vegetables. When the paste is spread evenly, fit the pieces into a quart (1 L) jar.

Allow to ferment at room temperature for 3 to 7 days. There is no need to apply weight to this ferment, since the fermentation period is so short.

Yield: 3 cups (675 g)

Ingredients

- 1 daikon or 1 pound (450 g) mixed radishes
- 2 tablespoons (38 g) kosher salt
- ½ cup (120 ml) filtered water
- 1 tablespoon (10 g) rice flour
- 4 cloves of garlic
- 2 inches (5 cm) of ginger
- 1 small onion, coarsely chopped
- ½ teaspoon fish sauce
- ¼ cup (30 g) gochugaru
- ½ bunch of Korean chives, trimmed

RADISH KIMCHI

The more traditional version of this kimchi would be made only with mu radish, but I enjoy the added zing that comes from using a variety of spicier radishes too. Feel free to go either route, depending on what you have access to and your preference for milder or zingier 'chi.

Cut the radishes into ¾-inch (2 cm) cubes. Place in a bowl and sprinkle the cut surfaces with salt. Let them sit for 30 minutes and then toss again, redistributing any residual salt at the bottom of the bowl.

Let them sit for another 30 minutes until visibly wet.

While the radishes are salting, bring the water and rice flour to a boil in your smallest saucepan, whisking constantly. Reduce the heat to medium and continue whisking until the mixture thickens, about 2 minutes. Remove from the heat and set aside to cool to room temperature.

Once the rice paste is cool and the radishes are damp, place the radishes in a colander and rinse thoroughly under cool water. Taste a radish. It should be quite salty but not inedible. Allow to drain.

Place the cooled rice paste, garlic, ginger, onion, fish sauce, and gochugaru into the bowl of a food processor and blend until a uniform paste forms.

Chop the chives into 2-inch (5 cm) pieces. Pat the radishes dry and place all the ingredients in a bowl. Put on your kimchi gloves and toss to combine. Once the vegetables are thoroughly coated in rice paste, pack them very tightly into a quart (1 L) jar. Wipe the rim of the jar with a clean, damp cloth to remove any paste that may have clung there. Loosely cover the jar with the lid and allow to ferment at room temperature from 7 days to 2 weeks.

Once you are happy with the flavor, secure the lid and place the jar in the fridge.

Yield: 1 quart (900 g)

Ingredients

- ½ small daikon
  (¼ pound, or 115 g)

- 1 pound (450 g)
  napa cabbage

- ¼ small onion (1 ounce, or
  25 g), chopped

- 1 small Asian pear (7 ounces,
  or 200 g), cored and cut
  into 8 pieces

- ½ inch (1.5 cm) of ginger,
  minced

- 1 carrot

- 2 scallions, trimmed and cut
  into 2-inch (5 cm) pieces

- 1 tablespoon (7.5 g) coarse
  gochugaru flakes

- 2 cloves of garlic, thinly
  sliced

- 5 teaspoons (28 g)
  kosher salt

- 4 cups (940 ml) filtered water

NABAK KIMCHI

The word *nabak* refers to the square shape of the vegetable pieces in this kimchi, but for me the defining characteristic of this particular kimchi is how it's eaten—as a delightfully light, chilled soup. Enjoy this kimchi as an appetizer when the seasons change from cold to warm.

Remove the daikon greens and crown. Cut the daikon into 1-inch (2.5 cm) thick rounds. To get the squarish, nabak shape, lay each round flat and cut into quarters. Slice each daikon quarter into ¼-inch (5 mm) thick squares. Repeat with each daikon slice, then with the carrot.

Mix the daikon, cabbage, onion, pear, ginger, carrot, scallions, gochugaru, and garlic together in a large bowl and then divide evenly between 2 quart (1 L) jars.

Mix the salt into the water until disolved and then pour the brine into each jar until the vegetables are just covered. Divide the gochugaru flakes between the jars and stir to distribute.

Although this is a brined ferment, the fermentation time is so short that submersion is not necessary. Ferment for 4 to 5 days and chill before serving.

Yield: 2 quarts (2 L)

RECIPE NOTE

Traditional nabak is brothier, but I prefer my soups to be loaded with veg. If you'd like to go the more traditional route, halve the amount of cabbage, daikon, scallions, and pear. Those who don't like heat can omit the gochugaru (red pepper flakes).

Ingredients

- 1¾ pound (790 g) head napa cabbage
- 1 daikon (9 ounces, or 250 g), trimmed, greens removed
- 2½ tablespoons (45 g) kosher salt
- 5 cups (1.2 L) filtered water
- 1¾ cups (42 g) tightly packed basil leaves
- 3 cloves of garlic
- 1½ teaspoons (7.5 g) brown sugar
- 2 tablespoons (7 g) red pepper flakes
- Zest of 2 lemons

PESTO-CHI

I never know exactly how many seeds will take in my garden, so I usually plant a lot more than I need, just to be safe. A few years ago, every seed took, and I ended up with several dozen basil plants. Unexpected bumper crops aren't always desirable when you have a limited container garden on your roof and two people in your family. As the season drew to a close, we had *really* eaten enough pesto, and the neighbors went a-runnin' when they saw me approaching with a fragrant bouquet. I knew it was time to find another use for my overgrowth. Thus was born pesto-chi, forever ending my search for ways to use an overabundance of basil.

Soak or thoroughly rinse the cabbage in room temperature water to remove any dirt and debris. Remove and reserve any unattractive or wilted outer leaves.

Halve the cabbage and remove the core. Slice each half into quarters. You will now have 8 long, 1½ inch (4 cm) wide strips of napa cabbage. Cut horizontally across each strip to create roughly 1½-inch (4 cm) squares. Place the cabbage pieces into a large bowl.

Slice the daikon into ¼- to ½-inch (5 mm to 1.5 cm) wide strips and cut them down to 2 to 3 inches (5 to 7.5 cm) in length, if necessary. Add to the bowl with the cabbage.

Add the salt to the water and stir to dissolve. Pour the brine into the bowl. Use a plate or another food-safe, nonmetallic item to keep the vegetables submerged under the brine. Cover the bowl with a kitchen towel and allow the vegetables to soak at room temperature for 12 to 24 hours. After soaking, drain the vegetables and pat dry.

Put the basil, garlic, brown sugar, and red pepper flakes in a food processor and blend to a paste consistency. Stir in the lemon zest.

Put on your kimchi gloves. Scoop the basil mixture into the bowl with the vegetables and use your hands to mix the ingredients together and to coat the vegetables. Once the ingredients are well mixed, remove the glove from your nondominant hand and use that hand to hold a clean quart (1 L) jar. Pack the jar tightly with kimchi.

Allow to ferment at room temperature from 5 days to 2 weeks. At 5 days, the basil flavor will be very prominent. The longer you ferment, the more it mellows into the sour flavors of fermentation.

Once you are happy with the flavor, remove the weight, secure the jar lid, and store in the fridge.

Yield: 1 quart (900 g)

Ingredients

- 1 head napa cabbage (1¾ pounds, or 800 g)
- 8 small cherry bell radishes, trimmed and quartered
- 1 carrot (2 ounces, or 50 g), chopped
- ¼ cup (75 g) kosher salt
- 8 cups (1.9 L) filtered water
- 1 large tomato (7 ounces, or 200 g)
- 2 tablespoons (32 g) tomato paste
- 2 large jalapeño peppers, stems and crowns removed
- ½ small onion (2 ounces, or 50 g)
- 3 cloves of garlic
- 4 scallions, chopped
- ½ bunch of cilantro, chopped (stems included)
- Zest of 1 lime

SALSA-CHI

My husband, a native Californian, made it his mission to introduce me to the best of what Central Coast taquerias had to offer. His taqueria campaign taught me that no taco is complete without a side of radish and carrot and the full complement of tasty salsas. Those flavors inspired this kimchi.

Soak or thoroughly rinse your cabbage in cool water to remove dirt and debris. Remove the wilted outer leaves. Halve the cabbage and remove the core. Slice each half into quarters. You will now have eight, 1½-inch (4 cm) wide strips. Cut horizontally across each strip to create roughly 1½-inch (4 cm) squares. Place all the cabbage pieces into a large bowl. Add the radish and carrot pieces.

Pour the salt into the water and stir to dissolve. Pour the brine over the vegetables in the bowl. Use a plate or another food-safe, nonmetallic item to keep the vegetables submerged under the brine. Cover the bowl with a kitchen towel and allow the vegetables to soak at room temperature for 12 to 24 hours. After soaking, thoroughly drain the vegetables and pat dry with a clean kitchen towel. Place in a large bowl.

Place the tomato, tomato paste, jalapeños, onion, and garlic into the bowl of a food processor and blend until smooth, scraping down as necessary. Once the mixture is smooth, pour it over the vegetables in the bowl. Add the scallions, cilantro, and lime zest to the bowl.

Put on your kimchi gloves and use your hands to mix the ingredients together and coat the vegetables. Once the ingredients are well mixed, remove the glove from your nondominant hand and use that hand to hold a clean quart (1 L) jar. Pack the mixture very tightly into the jar, cover the jar, and ferment at room temperature for 3 to 5 days.

Once you are happy with the flavor, secure the jar lid and store in the fridge.

Yield: 1 quart (900 g)

Ingredients

- ½ pound (225 g) green beans, ends trimmed
- 5 teaspoons (30 g) kosher salt
- 4½ cups (1.1 L) filtered water, divided
- 1 tablespoon (10 g) rice flour
- 1 inch (2.5 cm) of ginger, unpeeled
- ¼ cup (30 g) gochugaru
- 2 cloves of garlic
- ½ small (2 ounces, or 50 g) onion
- ½ teaspoon fish sauce
- ½ teaspoon Chinese 5-spice powder
- 5 stems of Chinese chives

GREEN BEAN KIMCHI

This is one of my very favorite kimchi creations. By no means a traditional kimchi, this recipe takes its inspiration from one of my favorite Chinese restaurant dishes—spicy green beans. The addition of Chinese five-spice powder is the key to a crazy flavorful dish.

Cut the green beans into 1-inch (2.5 cm) pieces and place in a bowl.

Mix the salt into 4 cups (940 ml) of the water and stir until dissolved. Pour the brine into the bowl with the green beans. Use a small plate or another food-safe, nonmetallic object to keep the beans submerged. Allow them to sit at room temperature overnight and then drain.

In your smallest saucepan, bring the remaining ½ cup (120 ml) water and the rice flour to a boil, whisking constantly. Reduce the heat to medium and continue whisking until the mixture thickens, about 2 minutes. Remove from the heat and allow to cool to room temperature.

Once the rice paste has cooled, put it in a food processor along with the ginger, gochugaru, garlic, onion, fish sauce, and 5-spice powder. Blend until smooth.

Put on your kimchi gloves. Scoop the blended rice paste into the bowl with the vegetables and use your hands to mix well and to coat the vegetables. Remove the glove from your nondominant hand and use that hand to hold a clean pint (500 ml) jar. Pack the mixture in the bowl tightly into the jar and then loosely attach the lid.

Allow to ferment at room temperature for 1 to 2 weeks. Once you're happy with the flavor, tighten the lid and store in the refrigerator.

Yield: 1 pint (450 kg)

CHAPTER FOUR

Sauces,
Salsas, and Condiments

The concept of eating pickled vegetables as an accompanient to virtually every meal has a long tradition in many cultures, from the Korean *banchan* to the Indian *thali*. In the West, we're more prone to cover a table in sauces and condiments as meal accompaniments. The recipes in this chapter seek to serve as a kind of combination of the two—why not get our probiotics while seasoning our foods the way we always do?

I know a lot of families have mixed values—half the family loves ferments while the other half says no thanks. Fermenting common condiments, however, can be a great way to lead more reluctant ferment consumers down the path to fermentation bliss.

Ingredients

- 4 medium ears of corn, preferably organic, shucked
- ½ cup (80 g) diced sweet onion
- ½ clove of garlic, thinly sliced
- 1 jalapeño pepper, diced
- 1½ teaspoons (12 g) coarse salt
- 1 cup plus 2 tablespoons (265 g) filtered water

SUMMER CORN SALSA

As a Michigan kid, I grew up with the sure knowledge that swimming pools + corn = summer. While you'll never convince me that the corn from any other state is as sweet, this salsa will make even lesser corn shine. It's a salsa that works great straight out of the jar or with the addition of some fresh chopped tomato and cilantro added just before serving. Don't worry about cooking the corn; fermentation will leave your corn barely sweet and ready to devour.

Place the wide end of one ear of corn on a plate or in a shallow bowl. Holding the other end, use a sharp knife to shave downward to remove the kernels from the cob. Repeat with the remaining ears.

Place the corn kernels, onion, garlic, and jalapeño into a pint (500 ml) jar. Mix the salt into the water and pour the brine over the vegetables. Using your preferred method (see pages 23 to 28), submerge your veggies and cover your jar.

Allow to ferment at room temperature for 4 to 5 days. The brine should be cloudy and the corn should still taste a little sweet. It should also be quite tangy.

Chill. Drain the fermenting liquid from the salsa before serving.

Yield: 1 pint (450 g)

Ingredients

1   heaping cup (200 g) cored chopped tomato (1 large heirloom or 3 medium slicers)

½   cup (75 g) chopped onion

1   small clove of garlic

½   jalapeño pepper, seeded

1   teaspoon (6 g) salt (or ¼ teaspoon for pico, plus more to taste in the finished product)

½   cup (8 g) packed fresh cilantro, stems and leaves

    Squeeze of lime (optional), for serving

SIMPLE SALSA, TWO WAYS

Since tomatoes are high in sugar, they can break down more quickly, resulting in an unpleasantly mealy feel rather than a fresh, ripe bite. For that reason, a puréed salsa is better if you are fermenting all of the ingredients. The other option is to skip the tomato during fermentation and add the fresh tomatoes and cilantro before serving (pico style). Both are tasty and quite different from one another. Serve with chips or tacos.

Puréed Style: Place the tomatoes, onion, garlic, and jalapeño in a pint jar (500 ml). Add the salt, put the lid on tightly, and give it a shake to distribute the salt. You should see the tomatoes giving up some liquid within a half hour. Loosen the lid a bit and set the over a towel or a plate in a spot out of direct sunlight.

Vegetable solids will rise to the top, so once or twice a day, give the jar a little shake to keep the tomatoes covered in liquid.

Taste at 3 days; if you like the flavor, it's done! If you think it could use a bit more acidity, give it another day.

Once it's fermented to your liking, strain off the liquid (you can reserve this to use as a starter for a condiment or add it to soup or anything else where you'd like a hit of acid, flavor, and salt). Place the contents of the jar in a food processor with all but 1 sprig of the cilantro. Pulse to get a slightly chunky texture.

Pour the salsa into a bowl and squeeze the lime over it. Chop the remaining cilantro and use as garnish.

Pico Style: Mince the garlic. Place the onion, garlic, and jalapeño in a pint (500 ml) jar. Mix a brine of ½ cup (120 ml) filtered water to ¼ teaspoon salt. Pour the brine over the veggies and secure the lid.

Allow to ferment at room temperature for 5 days.

Strain off the liquid and place fermented vegetables in a bowl. Toss with chopped tomatoes. Chop the cilantro and toss with the vegetables. Add salt to taste. Add a squeeze of lime if desired.

Yield: 1 pint (450 g)

Ingredients

1	bunch of cilantro, divided
40	mini or 10 regular tomatillos, husk removed, rinsed to remove stickiness
1	heaping teaspoon (4 g) minced white onion
1	small clove of garlic, minced
1½	teaspoons (9 g) kosher salt
1	cup (235 ml) filtered water

TOMATILLO SALSA

I live near the Italian Market in Philadelphia, dangerously close to a lot of iconic food shops. When I leave my door, I walk by countless vegetable stands, three cheese shops, a fantastic kitchen supply store, and, perhaps most tempting of all, Tortilleria San Roman. This pocket shop has hot fresh tortillas coming off the press all day long and a variety of house-made salsas. My favorite is their (unfermented) verde. The amount of salsa we've bought from there convinced me to start growing my own tomatillos so I could make my own fermented version. This is the result.

Place half of the bunch of cilantro in a pint (500 ml) jar. Top with the tomatillos, onion, and garlic. Stir the salt into the water and pour the brine into the jar. Close the jar with its lid, but leave the ring loose so that CO_2 can escape during fermentation.

Allow to ferment for 7 to 10 days and then strain off and reserve the liquid. Pulse the remaining half bunch of cilantro and the contents of the jar in a food processor until chunky. If you want a wetter salsa, add the reserved fermenting liquid a tablespoon (15 ml) at a time until you have the consistency you want. Serve immediately or store in the refrigerator.

Yield: 1 pint (450 g)

Ingredients

Cloves, star anise, mustard seeds, onion powder, etc., to taste (optional)

4 packed cups (400 g) hot peppers, stems and caps removed

5 cloves of garlic

1 tablespoon (18 g) salt

2 cups (470 ml) filtered water

HOT SAUCE

I may have come late to the hot sauce–making game, but once I started, I couldn't stop. I grow as many varieties of hot peppers as can fit on my roof, I buy them by the case from local farmers, and yet every year, my husband and I have cleaned out our varied stock of hot pepper sauces by February. This is a very flexible recipe. Substitute your favorite peppers for the Fresnos and cayennes that make my very favorite sauce.

If using seasonings, place in a pint jar (500 ml).

Slice the pepper in half lengthwise.

Pack the peppers and garlic into the jar, as tightly as possible. It's okay if the peppers break a bit.

Stir the salt into the water until dissolved. Pour the brine into the jar and use a weight ensure that the peppers stay submerged (see pages 23 to 28). You want to use as little brine as possible here, so be sure that your peppers are well packed in. Cover your jar.

Allow to ferment for at least 2 weeks. Peppers can ferment for quite a while. Over time, the heat will lessen somewhat, so for ferments that go longer than 3 months, be sure to use a bit more heat than you want in your final product. Peppers are prone to very cloudy brine and flakes in the brine and on the surface of the peppers. That is a normal part of the fermentation process and nothing to be concerned about. If the buildup is heavy, just quickly rinse the peppers in cool water before puréeing.

Once fermentation is complete, drain and reserve the brine and place the peppers and garlic in a food processor, straining out any whole spices prior to puréeing. Process for 2 to 3 minutes until a smooth paste forms.

Add the brine a tablespoon (15 ml) at a time until it reaches the desired consistency. For a liquid, Tabasco-style sauce, add it all. For a sriracha consistency, add between ¼ and ½ cup (60 and 120 ml) of brine.

Run the purée through a food mill or press through a fine-mesh strainer using a spatula. Reserve the paste to make Hot Pepper Flakes (page 134), if desired.

Pour into a bottle and store in the fridge.

Yield: 1 pint (500 ml)

Ingredients

Remaining paste from making 2 recipes of Hot Sauce (page 33), made as dry as possible through milling

HOT PEPPER FLAKES

Fermented red pepper flakes are a by-product of the hot sauce–making process. I love that these prevent food waste in a way that offers so much flavor for so long. You can definitely add your own house blend of super red pepper flakes to the list of tier one secret ingredients! If you have a dehydrator, you can keep these probiotic by keeping the temperature set to about 90°F (32°C). Otherwise, just bake them at the lowest setting in your oven.

Preheat the oven to 200°F (93°C).

On a large baking sheet lined with a silicone baking mat or parchment paper, spread the paste/seed mixture into a thin layer. Use a spatula to make the mix as uniform as possible. The thinner the layer, the faster it will dry in the oven.

Place the baking sheet in the oven and bake for about 2 hours until the paste is totally dried and crisp. You should be able to break a piece off. Set aside until cool and then break the chunks apart with clean fingers. Place them into a shaker or ½ pint (250 ml) jar. Store in the pantry or fridge.

Yield: 1 cup (225 g)

Ingredients

- 2 pounds (900 g) ripe tomatoes, preferably a fleshy heirloom variety
- 1 tablespoon (20 g) coarse sea salt
- 1 clove of garlic, coarsely chopped
- ½ medium onion (2 ounces, or 60 g), cut into chunks
- ¼ cup (10 g) packed fresh basil leaves
- 1 teaspoon (2 g) dried oregano
- Pinch of dried rosemary (optional)

FERMENTED TOMATO SAUCE

Tomatoes are usually fermented green (unripe) or with a starter because the texture of fermented ripe tomatoes is very mushy. In this case, however, you can go right for the ripest summer tomatoes. Since you'll be puréeing the final product, softness doesn't matter one bit. Fermenting ripe tomatoes results in an incredibly pure and intense tomato flavor. This concentrated flavor works best when lightly tossed with pasta or sautéed vegetables.

Chop the tomatoes into large chunks, removing the core and any wet seed clusters that are easy to push out. You should end up with about 4 cups (720 g) chopped tomatoes. Place in a bowl and toss with the salt.

Place the garlic and onion into a quart (1 L) jar and then add the salted tomatoes. The jar should be full up to the threads. Place the lid on the jar, but leave it a little loose so that CO_2 can escape during fermentation.

Allow to ferment at room temperature for 4 days, away from direct sunlight. The tomatoes and liquid will separate. Gently stir 1 to 2 times daily to re-submerge the vegetables and prevent surface yeasts from forming.

At 4 days, use a fine-mesh strainer to drain the liquid from the vegetables. If you want to reserve the liquid to use as braising liquid or soup stock, strain over a bowl and store in fridge.

Place the fermented vegetables, basil, oregano, and rosemary in a blender and process until very smooth. Use immediately or return to the jar and store in the fridge. This sauce will keep for at least 2 weeks, but it will become increasingly acidic as time passes.

Yield: 3 cups (735 g)

EGGPLANT PÂTÉ

This fermented spread makes a fantastic raw, vegan (if fish sauce is omitted), and gluten-free amuse-bouche when served on cucumber slices. If you want a little less fiber in your texture, carefully slice the peels off the eggplant after fermentation but before puréeing.

¾ pound (340 g) Italian eggplant, unpeeled

2 cloves of garlic

2¼ teaspoons (17 g) kosher salt

1½ cups (355 ml) filtered water

¼ cup (60 ml) olive oil

2 tablespoons (30 g) tahini

1 teaspoon (5 ml) fresh lemon juice

2 teaspoons (10 ml) fish sauce (optional)

Remove the ends of the eggplant and cut in half lengthwise. Cut each half into ½-inch (1.5 cm) slices.

Place the garlic cloves into a quart (1 L) jar and pack the eggplant slices on top.

Dissolve the salt into the water and pour the mixture over the vegetables in the jar. Using your preferred method (see pages 23 to 28), submerge the eggplant and cover your jar.

Allow to ferment for 1 week.

After fermentation, drain, reserving the liquid for another use, if desired. Remove the peels if a smoother pâté is desired.

Place the eggplant, garlic, olive oil, tahini, lemon juice, and fish sauce, if using, into a blender and blend on high until smooth. Scoop into a serving bowl and serve immediately or store in an airtight container in the fridge for up to 10 days. Note that the topmost layer may become discolored over time in the fridge; if that happens, just scrape off the top and enjoy what's underneath.

Yield: 1 heaping cup (240 g)

THOUSAND ISLAND DRESSING

Reubens may well be the fermentiest sandwich. Bread? Fermented. Cheese? Fermented. Sauerkraut? Fermented. Corned beef? Fermented. The only thing on the sandwich that isn't always fermented is the Thousand Island dressing. Here's the solution! Make your Thousand Island dressing with home fermented pickles and you complete the fermented picture. For an extra special Thousand Island dressing, sub Cumin Basil Beets (page 46) for cucumber pickles.

¼ cup (60 g) mayonnaise

2 tablespoons (30 g) ketchup

1 tablespoon (10 g) very finely minced Cocktail Onion Rings (page 66)

2 tablespoons (20 g) very finely minced Classic Dill Pickle Spears (page 68)

Mix all the ingredients together until a uniform, pink/peach color is achieved. Spoon or pour onto the sandwich of your choice. Any remaining dressing will keep in the fridge for a few days, but it may need to be stirred before using.

Yield: ½ cup (120 g)

Ingredients

- 1 small winter squash (1 pound, or 450 g), such as butternut, acorn, delicata, or kabocha

- 1½ teaspoons (9 g) kosher salt

- 1 cup (235 ml) filtered water

- ¼ cup (60 ml) olive oil

- ¼ cup (60 ml) pumpkin seed oil + 1½ teaspoons (7.5 ml) for drizzle (You can substitute walnut or hazelnut oil.)

- 2 tablespoons (30 ml) brine from fermentation of squash

- 2 tablespoons (30 g) tahini

- ½ cup (114 g) toasted pumpkin seeds

WINTER SQUASH HUMMUS

The first time I tasted the pickled butternut squash at a favorite Philly restaurant, CheU Noodle Bar, I knew the complexity of flavor meant it was fermented. The chef there, Ben Puchowitz, is often accessible behind the bar seating at CHeU, and he confirmed that it definitely doesn't mush during fermentation and that he makes it like a simple, brined lacto-pickle. I started making my own that night, and I've found it to be an extremely versatile pickle that goes very quickly. This dip makes it go even faster. Serve it with crispy, nutty crackers or raw and roasted carrots for dipping.

Peel the squash, reserving the larger strips of peel. Remove and discard the seeds and chop the squash into 1-inch (2.5 cm) chunks. Pack the pieces into a quart (1 L) jar and slide bits of the reserved peel in around the sides. Fit as much peel as you can into the jar, but skip the small pieces that will have to be weeded out after fermentation.

Stir the salt into the water and pour into the jar. Using your preferred method (see pages 23 to 28), weight the squash down and cover your jar.

Allow to ferment at room temperature for 6 days to 2 weeks. After fermentation, strain, but reserve 2 tablespoons (30 ml) of brine. Remove and discard the peel.

Place the squash, oils, and brine into a food processor and mix on high for 3 to 4 minutes, stopping the machine to scrape down the sides as necessary. The mixture should be quite smooth when it's done, so process for longer if necessary. Add the tahini and process for another minute until well combined.

Place in a bowl and use a spatula to smooth the surface. Drizzle with the remaining pumpkin seed oil and top with the pumpkin seeds.

Yield: 1½ cups (360 g)

CHAPTER FIVE

Kvass

Soda is too sugary, and beer and wine are too boozy. Coffee and tea may keep you buzzing all night long, and water, while great for hydrating our bodies, doesn't always wow our taste buds. So what are thirsty folks to do? Drink kvass! These fermented drinks push every health button, from vitamin and mineral content to probiotic pizazz, all while tasting great. Every vegetable has its own flavor signature. Some are fresh and acidify quickly, while others are earthy and funky. Many of these drinks can be made fizzy through bottling, if you're the bubble-loving type.

Kvass is traditionally made from beets, but any vegetable that ferments well will give you a top-notch beverage. Feel free to explore beyond the options you find here. Why not experiment with a holiday spice turnip kvass or a summer barbecue corn kvass?

Tips and Guidelines

Many of the general principles of fermentation laid out in part one apply here, but below are a few beverage-specific tips and guidelines.

Watch the Clock

Each recipe has a range of fermentation times. The earlier times will have a less infused flavor and lower acidity. If you're happy with the acidity at the earliest time in the range but you feel that it needs more flavor, move your jar to the refrigerator and allow it to continue to infuse for 10 days or more. The cooler temperature will slow fermentation, so the acidity won't increase much but the flavors of the vegetables and seasonings will continue to infuse.

As with all vegetable fermentation, temperature impacts fermentation time, so plan on tasting at the earlier part of the range in warmer homes or seasons and at the later part of the range at cooler times. You can absolutely go longer, but try to keep the temperature low. Over longer periods, you may see the formation of a thin layer of Kahm yeast (whitish in color and not fuzzy) on the surface, which is harmless. Just accept that Kahm is part of the process and skim off what you can when you see it.

Think Big (Jars)

Water-sealing crocks and large ½-gallon (1.9 L) jars work particularly well for these probiotic vegetable drinks. The jars are available most places that canning jars can be found.

Large European jars that seal with a gasket and clamp also make good choices (with a few caveats; see "A Literal Flavor Bomb," page 149) and are available in larger sizes, but old, store-bought pickle jars do the job quite well, too (just be sure to thoroughly clean them before use).

Get Visual

Some of these beverages will have boldly beautiful colors, while others will have a pale, cloudy appearance. That cloudiness is a normal part of the fermentation process and nothing to be concerned about, but if you want to amp up the hue a bit, add a few chunks of beet or a few sliced, red radishes to just about any kvass for a burst of color.

Let It Vent

CO_2 is created during all vegetable fermentation, and with kvass, it is especially important to make sure that it has a way to escape the fermentation vessel. If you own an airlock, this is a great place to use it. If you don't, make sure that the jar lid is attached loosely, so that air can't easily get in, but CO_2 can easily escape. Tightened lids could mean dangerous, exploding jars or messy, spraying kvass, neither of which is desirable. I always leave about 2 inches (5 cm) of space between the liquid and the rim of the jar, but as you can see in "Ask the Professional Kvass Maker," mine is not the only way to do it.

What's in a Name?

Kvass is a bit of a misnomer for these particular beverages because the word means "yeast" in a variety of languages, and the kind of fermentation we're doing here is primarily bacterial. The term kvass most accurately refers to bread kvass, a beer-like Russian ferment that is actually yeast-fermented.

So although the widely used word isn't technically correct, it can be considered somewhat accurate because these vegetable drinks are prone to that surface layer of yeast we just discussed (Kahm yeast). We know that that yeast layer is harmless and you may skim any stray bits you see, but I prefer to prevent the yeast from forming in the first place by giving my jar a daily swirl—not a hard shake, just a little swirl to disrupt the surface and prevent anything from forming there. If a yeast layer does somehow form, just skim it when you see it. These yeasts are more likely to occur during the warmer months, with sweeter vegetables (beets and carrots, for instance), and during longer fermentation periods. Even airlock systems will not keep surface yeasts from forming, so daily swirls are still recommended.

In addition to the swirl, I sometimes place a cabbage leaf or collard green into the opening of the jar. It can act as a surface barrier and also put any vegetables or seasonings that rise to the surface back underneath the liquid. For another perspective on dealing with Kahm, see "Ask a Professional Kvass Maker" on page 145.

RED BEET KVASS

This is my standard beet kvass recipe. I like to have a little on hand all year-round, substituting the basil for whatever herb is most seasonal when I start a batch. Beet kvass is also a daily favorite of my husband, who has found that it helps soothe his acid reflux. What I love most, though, is the luxurious, deep red color of this drink. It's perfect for Halloween parties and the *Buffy* lover in your life.

3 large beets (3 pounds, or 1.4 kg)

1 inch (2.5 cm) of ginger, grated

1 cup (24 g) whole basil stems

3 quarts (3 L) filtered water

1 to 2 teaspoons (6 to 12 g) salt (optional)

Remove the beet greens and wash the beets. Trim any unattractive bits of root and any soft spots and cut each beet into eighths.

Add the beets, ginger, and basil to a 1-gallon (4 L) jar. Pour the water in and cover the jar either with an airlock or with a lid left loose enough to allow CO_2 to escape.

Allow to ferment at room temperature for 6 to 10 days and then strain the liquid into a clean jar and chill before drinking.

Yield: 3 quarts (3 L)

SUNNY HERB KVASS

Urban gardening can require a bit of creativity, but herbs are always an easy option. I try to grow as many different types of herbs as I can fit, simply because they truly make the dish and because they're so inexpensive to grow. In the depth of summer, I make a few vats of this stuff to remind me that summer does exist on those cold, wintry December nights.

1 bunch of flat-leaf parsley

1 bunch of cilantro

1 bunch of basil

½ teaspoon (2 g) sea salt

3½ quarts (3.5 L) filtered water

Pick through the herb bunches, removing any yellowing or browning leaves.

Rinse the herbs and place the whole bunches and the salt into a 1-gallon (4 L) jar. Pour in the filtered water until the jar is full to 2 inches (5 cm) below the rim or fill all the way to the rim and place in a bowl for the duration of the fermentation.

Cover your jar, making sure it can vent CO_2, and allow to ferment at room temperature for 5 to 6 days. Strain the liquid into a clean jar and chill before drinking.

Yield: 3½ quarts (3.5 L)

Ask a Professional Kvass Maker

Carly and Dave Dougherty are the owners of Food & Ferments, an upstate New York-and Philadelphia-based fermentation company. Food & Ferments is beloved for innovative kombucha and kraut flavors and most especially for a beet kvass that has fans all over the East Coast. Although in their commercial operation they have specialized equipment that prevents Kahm yeast from forming on the surface of the kvass they sell, they are no strangers to Kahm in their home production. Here are a few of Carly's top tips for perfect kvass.

ON AVOIDING KAHM YEASTS ON BEET KVASS

- **Fill jars all the way to the top,** so that the liquid makes contact with the lid. Store the jar over a plate or bowl during fermentation because it may bubble over, but it's worth it to avoid the off flavors that can sometimes result from Kahm yeast.
- **Use an airlock for home production.** This is the one instance where an airlock may make sense for home fermentation. The less air exposure, the less likely you are to see a Kahm layer pop up. If the kvass bubbles out so much that the level in the jar lowers below the lid, simply add a bit more water to refresh and reseal the kvass's contact with the lid. In the first few days, when the beet kvass is most active, your airlock may fill with kvass as it expands. Don't worry; refill your airlock with fresh water (or, better yet, vodka to prevent unwanted microbial activity in the airlock) after the activity has ceased, usually within 4 days or so.

ON CONCOCTING KVASS

- **Spice it up.** Many beet kvass recipes use just beets, salt, water, and maybe a little whey. For best results, spice it up! Adding pungent roots and spicy peppers to beet kvass is a good way to make the flavor more savory and refreshing. Ginger, garlic, horseradish, and jalapeño are all excellent additions.
- **Go long.** Remember that your kvass will develop more flavor and acidity the longer it's fermented. Carly and Dave ferment their kvass for 3 to 4 weeks, which may be one reason that it's a favorite for so many of their patrons.

FINAL THOUGHTS

If you do get Kahm yeast on your home-brewed kvass, it's really not a big deal. Skim it off when you see it and enjoy the finished ferment when it's ready.

<< WINTER HERB KVASS

The city of Geneva, Switzerland, might as well be the set of a spaghetti western for the number of tumbleweeds that roll through town during ski season. With snow falling in the nearby Alps, residents flee to the hills, snowboards and skis in hand. I've never enjoyed being cold or falling on my butt, so my go-to activity when I lived in Geneva was to accompany friends up the hill. While they skied, I hiked through the snowy pines and soaked up the winter sun. Each intensely herbaceous and woody gulp of this kvass reminds me of pine trees and sunshine on the chilly slopes.

1 large radish, cut into thirds

1 large bunch (2 ounces, or 60 g) of fresh thyme

1 large bunch (2 ounces, 60 g) of fresh rosemary

1 large bunch (2 ounces, 60 g) of fresh sage

¼ teaspoon sea salt

3 quarts (3 L) filtered water

Place the radish, whole herb bunches, and salt into a 1-gallon (4 L) jar and pour the filtered water in until the jar is full to 2 inches (5 cm) below the rim or fill all the way to the rim and place in a bowl for the entirety of the fermentation. Cover your jar, making sure it can vent CO_2, and leave to ferment at room temperature for 5 to 7 days. Strain the liquid into a clean jar and chill before drinking. This mixture may be fermented for longer than 7 days, but the flavor starts to become quite woody.

Yield: 3 quarts (3 L)

WOODSY GIN AND TONIC

When I let my Winter Herb Kvass ferment a bit too long and the woodsy flavor becomes a bit too intense to enjoy as a stand-alone drink, I know it's time to break out the gin. I'm all about serving up the secret ingredients to impress guests, and this mixer will definitely have them wondering how you make your G&Ts better than everyone else's.

¼ cup (60 ml) gin

2 tablespoons (30 ml) Winter Herb Kvass

⅓ cup (80 ml) tonic water

Twist of lime

Pour the gin and kvass into a Collins glass full of ice. Add the tonic water and garnish with a twist of lime.

Yield: 1 cocktail

Ingredients

- 4 large Chioggia beets
  (4 pounds, or 1.8 kg)

- 2 organic unwaxed
  lemons, quartered

- 8 inches (20 cm) of ginger,
  unpeeled, chopped

- 1 tablespoon (5 g)
  coriander seeds

- 4 bay leaves

- 2 allspice berries

- 4 juniper berries

- 1 teaspoon salt (optional)

- 9 cups (2.1 L)
  filtered water

BULL'S-EYE BEET KVASS

I love to make kvass with the Chioggia beets. Their interior bull's-eye pattern is eye candy during fermentation, but better yet, they make a straight-up neon beverage. I love that it's not just weird food dyes and insane processing methods that can make a bright pink drink. I relish the knowledge that something can be organic, healthful, and this colorful. If you can't find Chioggia beets, feel free to use golden or red beets instead. The only difference will be the color.

Remove the crown and greens from the beets. Trim any unattractive bits of root and any soft spots and cut each beet into eighths. Scrub and quarter the lemons. Put the ginger, coriander, bay leaves, allspice berries, juniper berries, and salt in a 1-gallon (4 L) jar, add the beets and unsqueezed lemon wedges, and pour in the filtered water to fill to 2 inches (5 cm) below the rim. Cover your jar, making sure it can vent CO_2, and leave to ferment at room temperature for 7 to 10 days. Strain the liquid into a clean jar and chill before drinking.

Yield: 9 cups (2.1 L)

RECIPE NOTE You can do a second batch with the same vegetables and seasonings. The flavor will be completely different and the color will not be as intense. The second batch will only need to ferment for 3 days.

A Literal Flavor Bomb

I frequently ferment kvass in Euro-style clamp-and-gasket jars. They are sold in 4- and 5-liter sizes and they don't seem to get Kahm on the surface quite as frequently as mason jar batches do. Having said that, any jar that seals should be used with caution. Although it's a rare issue with kvass, which doesn't bubble quite as much as yeast-fermented beverages do, sealed jars can explode when too much pressure builds up from the CO_2 created during fermentation. So, if you decide to use a sealing jar for beverage fermentation, and especially if it's glass, be aware of the explosion risk and take preventive and protective measures. Here are a few tricks I use:

- Never fill a gasket-sealing jar all the way to the lid. That is the path to in-home kvass sprinklers.
- Burp (aka open) the jar every few days.
- Ferment for a short time (3 to 5 days) and then move to the fridge for 1 to 2 weeks of low and slow fermentation.
- Keep the jar in a cooler or a double paper bag inside of a plastic bag.

LETTUCE KVASS

Students in my fermentation classes frequently ask whether there are any vegetables you can't ferment. In answer, I point to lettuce kvass (a ferment I initially discovered through Sandor Ellix Katz's book *The Art of Fermentation*) as proof that, if you're willing to be creative, you can ferment almost any vegetable. Lettuce isn't the most vigorous fermenter in my experience, so the addition of lots of herbs and other seasonings is what really makes this pickled sip a success.

1 head of iceberg lettuce, quartered

1 shallot (15 g), peeled and sliced in half

1 large bunch of dill, stems trimmed

4 juniper berries

1 teaspoon (4 g) mustard seed

1 teaspoon (2 g) peppercorns

½ bunch (15 g) of mint

2 quarts (2 L) filtered water

1 to 2 teaspoons (6 to 12 g) salt (optional)

Make sure that the lettuce is fresh and that any soft, brown, or orangish pieces have been removed.

Place all the seasonings into a 1-gallon (4 L) jar and add the lettuce halves. Pour in the filtered water until the jar is filled to 2 inches (5 cm) below the rim. Cover your jar, making sure it can vent CO_2.

Let it ferment at room temperature for 5 to 8 days. If the lettuce has begun to brown, time's up!

Strain the liquid into a clean jar and chill before drinking.

Yield: 2 quarts (2 L)

CABBAGE KVASS

I highly recommend drinking the sauerkraut juice that is left in the jar once you've eaten a batch. This cabbage kvass is a bit of a shortcut to that tasty, probiotic juice and one that was inspired by a trip to my favorite Eastern European grocery store, Net Cost Market, in northeast Philly. Net Cost has an inspiring pickle bar that usually includes a vat of pickled cabbage liquid. This recipe is my homage to that, but if you want to be more authentic, add three or four hot peppers for a very spicy batch.

½ head of red cabbage (1¼ pounds, or 560 g)

½ small red onion (2 ounces, or 50 g), peeled and halved

2 cloves of garlic, peeled and halved

2 tablespoons (14 g) caraway seeds

3½ quarts (3.5 L) filtered water

1 to 2 teaspoons (6 to 12 g) salt

Cut the cabbage into quarters.

Place the onion, garlic, and caraway seeds into a 1-gallon (4 L) jar and place the cabbage pieces on top.

Pour the filtered water over the ingredients until the jar is full to 2 inches (5 cm) below the rim or fill all the way to the rim and place the jar in a bowl for the duration of fermentation.

Cover your jar, ensure that it can vent CO_2, and let it ferment at room temperature for 5 to 10 days.

Strain liquid into a clean jar and chill before drinking.

Yield: 3½ quarts (3.5 L)

Ingredients

1 bunch of celery
(1¼ pounds, or 560 g)

Three 2-inch (5 cm) sprigs of
fresh thyme

½ teaspoon (1 g) celery
seeds

2 bay leaves

1 teaspoon (2 g)
peppercorns

1 yellow core of lemon-
grass, split lengthwise

¼ teaspoon cayenne
pepper

3 quarts (3 L) filtered
water

1 to 2 teaspoons (6 to 12 g)
salt (optional)

CELERY KVASS

My husband is a kvass lover, and this might be his favorite of all the vegetable kvasses I make. It captures all of the fresh green notes of the celery but has none of the bitterness. Pour it over ice in a highball glass and garnish with a sprig of thyme for a nonalcoholic cocktail that will impress.

Rinse the celery stalks thoroughly to remove any dirt. Trim the ends, but do not remove the leaves. Cut each stalk into thirds.

Place all the seasonings into a 1-gallon (4 L) jar and add the celery. Pour in the filtered water, filling the jar to 1 to 2 inches (2.5 to 5 cm) from the rim or fill all the way to the rim and place over a bowl for the duration of the fermentation period.

Cover your jar, making sure it can vent CO_2, and leave to ferment at room temperature for 5 to 9 days.

Strain the liquid into a clean jar and chill before drinking.

Yield: 3 quarts (3 L)

Ingredients

1 large cucumber

1 fennel bulb, with fronds

Peel of ½ an orange, no pith

3 quarts (3 L) filtered water

1 teaspoon (6 g) salt (optional)

CUCUMBER FENNEL KVASS

Although fermented vegetable drinks may not be the preferred option for ladies who lunch, I believe this is an option that could tempt even the most elegant and choosy of the spa-going set. The fennel dominates and is rounded out by the fresh cucumber notes. This is one I have no problem serving at a summer tea party.

Cut the cucumber into 1-inch (2.5 cm) thick slices. Chop the fennel bulb into large chunks and separate each frond from the bulb. When peeling the orange, cut strips that are as long as possible; avoid pith as it will impart an unpleasantly bitter aftertaste. Place the cucumber, fennel, and orange peel in a 1-gallon (4 L) jar and pour the filtered water in until the jar is full to 2 inches (5 cm) below the rim or fill all the way to the rim and place in a bowl for the duration of the fermentation period. Cover your jar, making sure it can vent CO_2, and leave to ferment at room temperature for 5 to 10 days.

Once it tastes sufficiently flavorful and acidic, strain the liquid into a clean jar and chill before drinking.

Yield: 3 quarts (3 L)

Ingredients

- 15 purple carrots (2 pounds, or 900 g)
- 3 whole star anise
- 2 cinnamon sticks
- 3 inches (7.5 cm) of ginger, cut into ¼-inch (5 mm) slices
- 1 tablespoon (6 g) cumin seeds
- 1 teaspoon (2 g) peppercorns
- 10 raisins
- Peel of 1 small lemon, no pith
- Peel of 1 small lime, no pith
- Peel of half an orange, no pith
- 11 cups (2.6 L) filtered water
- 1 to 2 teaspoons (6 to 12 g) salt

MOROCCAN CARROT KVASS

When I was a kid, I saved up my babysitting money and lobbied my generous parents to let me spend a few summers in southwestern France. The first time my French host family took me to a Moroccan restaurant, my taste buds danced. I could not believe how perfectly the sweet and savory flavors played off of each other. Ever since, I've loved cooking with the sweet and savory seasonings of Moroccan cuisine. Make this with purple-skinned carrots for a color that resembles the pink-orange sunsets of Morocco, but orange carrots are a fine substitute for flavor.

Trim the carrots and cut them into 2-inch (5 cm) cylinders.

Add the star anise, cinnamon, ginger, cumin, peppercorns, raisins, and citrus peels to a 1-gallon (4 L) jar and place the carrots on top. Pour the filtered water in until the jar is full to 2 inches (5 cm) below the rim or fill all the way to the rim and place in a bowl for the duration of the fermentation period.

Cover your jar, making sure it can vent CO_2, and leave to ferment at room temperature for 5 days to 2 weeks.

Once it tastes sufficiently flavorful and acidic, strain the liquid into a clean jar and chill before drinking.

Yield: 11 cups (2.6 L)

PART

3

Alternative Approaches to Vegetable Fermentation

Remember all those rules we laid out in part one? Well, you may need to press pause on those while you work through this section. Many of the important details applied in previous chapters (salt levels, not peeling, submersion, small batches) will be set aside in one or more of the recipes and techniques outlined here. Get ready for a glimpse into the wide world of ferments that go way beyond simple salt and vegetables in a jar!

CHAPTER SIX

Fermenting in Crocks

Crocks are great for preserving a larger harvest (or for taking advantage of a great bulk deal at the farmers' market). The basic principles of vegetable fermentation apply equally to jar and crock fermentation, but sizing up to crocks does offer unique opportunities and challenges.

Tips and Guidelines

Most of the general principles of fermentation laid out in part one apply to the recipes in this chapter, but there are few additional points to take into account.

Choose the Right Crock for You

There are two primary types of ceramic crocks available in the West. Each has advantages and disadvantages to consider before purchase.

WATER-SEALED CROCKS

Water-sealed crocks, sometimes referred to under the brand name Harsch crocks, make for a very easy ferment. They are generally more expensive than their open crock counterparts, but they come with a lid and often with weights that create the perfect fermentation barrier. No air enters the crock once the water "seal" is poured, but CO_2 created during fermentation easily bubbles out. Batches made in water-sealed crocks rarely accrue a layer of Kahm yeast during fermentation. They can be somewhat challenging to clean after fermentation, depending on their size.

Ideal for: This crock is ideal for fermenters with a deep and abiding (though let's be honest: illogical) fear of surface molds or yeasts; fermenters who want to set it and forget it; fermenters who want to create larger batches of favorite jarred ferments. It's perfect for Simplest Sauerkraut (page 76) or Classic Cukes (page 162).

Special tip: Check the moat around your crock about once a week to make sure there's still water in there. If it seems a bit low, top it off with fresh water. If the moat dries out completely, the seal will be broken and air will be allowed to flow into your crock. Opening the crock also lets air in, so it's better to keep the lid on until the end of fermentation when using a water-sealed crock.

OPEN CROCKS

Open crocks are usually less expensive than water-sealed crocks and their wide, cylindrical shapes make it easy to fit in and position a variety of larger pieces and whole vegetables. Weights and lids often need to be purchased separately and can dramatically raise the cost of an open crock. Open crocks that are not covered with a fitted lid and left undisturbed are prone to developing a layer of Kahm yeast, the harmless yeast that appears when a ferment is exposed to the air. Depending on their size, open crocks are quite easy to clean, since their bases and openings are the same diameter.

Ideal for: This crock is ideal for farmers and those with a large garden. It's perfect for fermenting whole vegetable recipes such as Sauerkraut Steak (page 174) and whole heads of Crock Kimchi (page 170).

Special tip: It's better to start open crock batches, especially with whole vegetables or larger pieces, during cooler periods to avoid surface yeasts. Even during normal or cool temperature periods, checking the surface of the crock every few days and skimming off any Kahm yeast that may have appeared on the surface is a good bet. Kahm isn't harmful, but if mold forms in a thick layer, it imparts unpleasant flavors and can cause issues with acidity, which would be problematic. If you develop true mold (that isn't colorful), it's not necessarily a reason to throw out the contents of your crock. Skim the mold, ladle some brine or veg from as deep in the crock as possible, and use a pH strip to test acidity. If the pH is 4.0 or below (as measured with a strip), you may safely eat the vegetables in the crock if they taste good!

Weigh Your Salt

When fermenting in crocks, accurate salt measurements becomes more important.

When salting vegetables for the jar, measuring rather than weighing is a totally reasonable choice. While measuring may result in a gram or three of difference for a jar, the larger scale of crock fermentation makes these "small" variations that occur between measuring vs. weighing and using one salt type vs. another much more pronounced. Furthermore, inconsistent salt levels for smaller batches have low stakes. If you use a little too much or too little and your pint of pickles is too salty or too soft, it's not that big of a loss. If you've filled a crock with 45 pounds (20 kg) of cabbage, on the other hand, you might be a bit more peeved if that particular batch doesn't turn out.

If you've invested in a crock, investing a small amount in a digital gram scale may well be worth it for the accuracy it provides. If you are an experienced fermenter, accustomed to salting to taste, you can absolutely continue that practice in crock fermentation.

Use Weights

For most things you'll put in your crock, a heavy weight is very useful. If you're selecting household items or crafting your own, remember that materials that don't corrode, get moldy, or expand when wet are your best options. Avoid wood and metal and make sure that your weight fits comfortably through the narrowest part of your crock. Things move around during fermentation and a weight that's too large could potentially damage your crock.

Tannins

Tannins added to a batch of pickles can make all the difference between crispy and floppy. There are several safe sources of tannins that you can add to your pickles for crisp and crunch.

- **Grape leaves.** Grape leaves are my go-to source for tannins. They are easily found in most grocery stores, and they do not impart flavor or bitterness. They do the work of keeping pickles crispy quite well. If buying pre-salted leaves, soak them in room temperature water first to leech out some of the salt.
- **Tea.** Black tea is the best choice from a crispness standpoint, but it also imparts the most flavor. Sometimes that's a plus, but consider whether it's a good fit for the particular recipe.
- **Berry leaves (raspberry, blackberry, or strawberry).** Raspberry leaves are the best berry tannin option I've found. They work wonderfully but are challenging to find if you don't grow your own raspberries.
- **Red wine.** Wine works well in small doses, but it should not be used in quantity because the alcohol can have a negative impact on lactic acid bacteria. Small doses are fine, but I've had the best luck using a maximum of 1 tablespoon (15 ml) per pint (500 ml) of pickles.
- **Hops.** Hops impart flavor and a bit of their characteristic bitterness, but they do help keep veggies from softening.
- **Rosehips.** The fruit of the rose plant is known for its high vitamin C content, but it is also very high in tannins. It imparts quite a bit of bitterness, so it is best used as a tannin source of last resort or in a pickle where added bitterness could be a plus.

From Crock to Jar

Once a crock ferment is finished fermenting, the fun part begins—eating it! Only maybe you have just two or four people in your family. And even if all of those people love sauerkraut/pickled onions/kimchi, you're unlikely to be able to work through the contents of a crock within a few days. If that's the case, you have options, including any combination of the following:

- **Store it in the cellar.** Sadly, most of us don't have root cellars and many of us don't have basements. Even for those who do, crocks can be unwieldy, and full crocks can be downright back-breaking (or impossible) to carry. This option works best for small crocks. Ferments in open crocks can pick up some musty basement aromas, so water-sealed crocks are a better choice for basement storage. Once you've put your crock into the cooler climes, you can remove small amounts to store in the fridge (in a jar) and consume. If your basement stays below 60°F (15.6°C), consider a very long, slow fermentation period in a large crock that starts and ends down in the basement.

- **Transfer to jar.** Transferring to a jar for fridge storage is a great option—provided you have the fridge space. With brined ferments, use a fork or slotted spoon to transfer the vegetables to one or more large jars, and then use a ladle to add a sufficient amount of brine to each jar so that the vegetables are covered. Close the jar and place in the fridge. It is very likely there will be a good amount of brine left in the crock.

- **Eat it from the crock.** Eating ferments right out of the crock may well be the easiest way to enjoy crock-fermented foods. Having said that, it does have its pitfalls. Every time you open your crock or remove the weights, you're exposing your ferment to the air and increasing the chance that you will end up with some sort of surface activity (mold or yeast) as a result. Additionally, when left at room temperature, your vegetables will continue to ferment, becoming more acidic as the days, weeks, or months pass. If you decide to go this route, keep the crock in a cool place and be sure to only use clean utensils to pull edibles from your crock (and no double dipping)!

It's really a matter of finding a balance and figuring out what works for you. There's no wrong answer, and a mix of methods can work wonderfully. Try jarring as much as you can reasonably store in the fridge and give to friends while continuing to eat small amounts from the crock.

Ingredients

Per gallon (3.8 L) of crock space:

4 to 7	pounds (1.8 to 3.2 kg) Kirby or pickling cucumbers, depending on the size of the cucumbers
4	bulbs of garlic
1	large onion, peeled and quartered
10	dill heads or 3 large bunches of fresh dill
¾	cup (135 g) mustard seeds
1	cup (70 g) packed grape leaves (see page 160 Tannins, for other options)
6	tablespoons (110 g) kosher salt
2	quarts (2 L) filtered water

CLASSIC CUKES

This is how I prefer to make cucumber pickles. Although I recommend moving them to the fridge after fermentation for best results, I cannot tell a lie: I often leave my crock full o' pickles at room temperature and just fish them out (with clean utentsils!) as needed, until I'm down to the very end of the batch. Kahm forms, but otherwise it works just fine that way, probably because these sign-of-summer pickles never last long. If this is your first crock batch, take the fridge route. But once you've got the hang of it, they're great as crock snacks.

Trim the thinnest possible layer from each end of the cucumbers, and then place them in a large bowl of ice water. While the cukes are soaking, peel the garlic. This is a lot of garlic, so don't worry about getting every little papery piece of peel off.

Place the garlic, onion, dill, mustard seeds, and grape leaves in the crock. Drain the cucumbers and pack them into the crock, leaving about 4 inches (10 cm) at the top of the crock for the weights. Apply the weights.

Stir the salt into the water until dissolved and then pour the brine into the crock, covering the cukes with 1 inch (2.5 cm) of brine. Cover the crock.

Allow to ferment for 3 to 7 days. If the seasonings don't seem fully infused, pack the pickles into jars, pour in the brine and seasonings from the crock, and move them to a cooler place like the cellar or refrigerator. Allow them to infuse for an additional 7 to 10 days before enjoying. Or, taste one a day until they're just right and then have a pickle feast.

Yield: 1 gallon (3.8 L)

RECIPE NOTE You may need more or less brine depending on your crock and vegetables. Use a concentration of 1½ tablespoons (27 g) kosher salt per 2 cups (470 ml) filtered water for 6% brine.

Ingredients

Per gallon (3.8 L) of crock space:

2 to 3 bunches of collard greens (2 to 3 pounds, or 900 to 1350 g), depending on the size of the leaves

¼ cup (64 g) kosher salt

2 quarts (2 L) filtered water

WHOLE LEAF COLLARD GREENS

This is the rare, quick crock ferment. Fermented collard greens taste so very delicious, but if they ferment for too long, they end up mushy and rotted. These leaves make awesome, naturally gluten-free wraps great for paleos and vegans alike. They are super flavorful but also salty, so choose wrap ingredients that are salt-free or low salt.

Cut off the part of the stems that protrude below the leaf, reserving them for another use (they pickle nicely on their own). Carefully wash the collard leaves and remove any blemished leaves and cut out any wet, mushy, dark green spots. Reserve 2 leaves for topping the crock.

Lay the leaves flat on top of each other and divide them into 2 piles. Loosely roll the piles up like rugs and stand them on their sides in the crock. If you have trouble rolling the leaves, you can shave a bit off the back of the stems to make the leaves more flexible. Do not overpack the crock. Overpacking can damage the leaves, making individual leaves difficult to remove from the crock and resulting in a mushy ferment.

Stir the salt into the water until dissolved and then pour the brine over the collards. Place the reserved collard leaves on top, submerging them in the brine as well. Apply a light weight, such as a small bowl or plate, and cover the crock. Standard crock weights will compress the collards too much, resulting in some mushy spots.

Allow to ferment 4 to 5 days at room temperature. Enjoy the collards soon after fermentation or store in the refrigerator, covered in brine from the crock (a larger, rectangular food storage container with a tight-fitting lid works well for this) for up to 3 days. Pat dry before using.

Yield: Approximately 25 collard leaves

- Look for unblemished leaves that are roughly the same size.

- You may need more or less brine depending on your crock and vegetables. Use a concentration of 1 tablespoon (16 g) kosher salt per 2 cups (470 ml) filtered water for a 3.5% brine.

Ask a Professional Potter

I asked Jeremy Ogusky, the Boston-based potter behind claycrocks.com and the Boston Fermentation Festival, a few questions about how best to find and care for crocks. He shares a bit of his knowledge below.

ON USING OLDER CROCKS

Safety first. Lead is unlikely to be an issue in U.S. pottery made in the last 100 years; however, some pottery from Mexico may contain glazes that are unsafe for food use. To test the viability of glaze on a crock of unknown origins, leave a lemon slice or some distilled white vinegar in the crock overnight. If there is a change in the color or the texture of the glaze, it is reactive and the crock is not suitable for fermentation. You should also run your hand along the crock to see if the glaze is smooth. If the glaze looks or feels rough, that crock isn't a great choice. Rough glaze could indicate the presence of microscopic pockets where microbes can set up shop and refuse to leave, causing unwanted funkiness in your finished ferments over time.

ON WHAT TO LOOK FOR IN A NEW CROCK

Look for a thicker crock. It will provide better insulation, which helps regulate temperature. Clay is a nonreactive and relatively cheap material that does a great job of insulating—that's one good reason it's been used to make fermenting vessels for thousands of years.

ON FUNCTION AND FORM

Whether buying new or used, observe the interior and exterior of the crock. Do you see any cracks? When you run your hand over the crock, do you feel any cracks or divots? If so, it's not a great choice.

To test for leaks, put some water in it; it must be watertight. Water could leak if the stoneware has a crack. Earthenware crocks, for instance, aren't suitable for vegetable fermentation because they are not watertight.

ON TERMINOLOGY

On commercially produced crocks, you'll see the words "High-Fired at × degrees to vitrification." Vitrification means the clay itself has gone through a chemical transformation so that it is no longer porous. A porous crock could slowly lose liquid over time and might harbor bacteria even after thorough cleaning.

A glaze is an exterior surface that is bonded to clay during firing. Glaze serves the dual purpose of beautifying and protecting the clay.

ON CLEANING CROCKS

Crocks are easy to clean. Some crocks are dishwasher safe (check your manual first), but a hand wash with soap and water is usually best. No scouring is required.

If there was mold in your crock, it may be worth doing a wipe down of the interior of the crock with a 50 percent bleach solution and then rinsing thoroughly before the next use.

FINAL THOUGHTS

Although crocks are great for fermenting, you don't need to buy any specialized equipment to ferment vegetables. You don't even need a crock to get started. Start fermenting with whatever you have access to and upgrade to a crock when it makes sense for you.

Ingredients

1 avocado

2 hard-boiled eggs

½ bell pepper

2 Whole Leaf Collard Greens (page 164)

3 handfuls arugula or other spicy salad mix

2 tablespoons (30 ml) Thousand Island Dressing (page 137, optional)

COLLARD WRAPS

This simple, gluten-free, paleo-friendly wrap is what I eat for lunch most days. It's loaded with protein and good fats and definitely gives me tons of energy. I used to have that 2 p.m. slump, but this veggie-powered lunch pushes me right through the afternoon yawns. Vegans can substitute unsalted, cooked tempeh and/or hummus for egg, as I often do.

Peel the avocado and eggs. In a small bowl, mash the avocado with a fork. Cut the egg into thin rounds and the bell pepper into thin strips. Lay the collards flat on a plate. Scoop half of the mashed avocado into the middle of each collard leaf.

Divide the arugula evenly between the collards. Press it into the avocado a bit and top with the pepper slices. Layer on the egg slices and drizzle with the dressing, if using.

Fold the outer edges of each side of the leaf into the center and then do the same with the top and bottom edges. Eat with your hands.

Yield: 2 wraps

Ingredients

*Per 2.6 gallons (10 L)
of crock space:*

- 12 pounds (5.4 kg) smallish onions (4 to 6 ounces, or 115 to 170 g each)

- ½ cup (88 g) mustard seeds

- ¼ cup (20 g) coriander seeds

- 3 cinnamon sticks

- 7 bay leaves

- 5 allspice berries

- 5 juniper berries

- 3 cinnamon sticks

- 3 whole star anise

- 3 tablespoons (15 g) peppercorns

- 2 tablespoon (4 g) dill seeds

- 1 tablespoon (6 g) red pepper flakes

- 2 cloves of garlic

- 1 cup plus 1½ teaspoons (330 g) kosher salt

- 5¾ quarts (5.8 L) filtered water

WHOLE ONIONS

Whole pickled onions are good eatin': they can be stuffed, sliced thin to top salads, or, if you want to freak someone out, eaten whole like an apple. At one month of fermentation, small onions will have a killer flavor—a true balance between sweet and sour. The longer they ferment, the more sour they become. If you're looking to cook them, slice thin and sauté for effortlessly crispy rings.

Peel the onions. Place all the spices and the garlic into the crock.

Fit the onions into the crock, starting with the largest onions and ending with the smallest. When all the onions are in the crock, place the weights on top. There should be sufficient space for your weights to fit on top with 2 inches (5 cm) of headspace. You may need to maneuver the onions so that everything fits.

Stir the salt into the water until dissolved. Pour the brine into the crock. In a water-sealed crock, there should be a brine layer of a ½ to 1 inch (1.5 to 2.5 cm) above the onions. If you're working in an open crock, you will want a 2-inch (5 cm) brine layer if possible because evaporation will reduce brine during fermentation. If the crock is too full to allow for a 2-inch (5 cm) brine layer, check every week and top off the brine if necessary.

Allow to ferment at room temperature for 1 to 3 months.

Once the onions are as sour as you'd like, you can move them all to jars and put them in cold storage (cellar or fridge).

Yield: 2 gallons (7.6 L)

The amount of brine will vary based on the size of your onions; 1 to 1½ gallons (3.8 to 5.7 L) is average. Use a concentration of 2 teaspoons (14 g) kosher salt per 1 cup (235 ml) filtered water for a 6% brine.

Ingredients

Per 3 gallons (11.4 L) of crock space:

- 6 to 8 small heads napa cabbage (12 pounds, or 5.5 kg)
- ¾ cup (225 g) kosher salt
- 4 quarts and 3 cups (4.5 L) filtered water, divided
- 6 tablespoons (60 g) rice flour
- 2 large daikon (4 pounds, or 1.8 kg), greens removed
- 2 large bunches of Korean chives (1 pound, or 450 g), trimmed
- 1 whole ginger rhizome, thoroughly washed and trimmed (left unpeeled)
- 2 bulbs of garlic, peeled
- 2 small onions, peeled
- ½ cup (120 ml) fish sauce
- ¼ cup (32 g) drained salted shrimp (saewoo juht)
- 4½ cups (540 g) gochugaru

CROCK KIMCHI

I LOVE crock kimchi. I have no science-based explanation, but to me, it always tastes better from the crock than from the jar. Plus, whole heads of kimchi make knockout food gifts for the pepperhead in your circle. Just put it in a pretty container and tie it up with a bow. Since kimchi is not usually prone to surface yeast issues, I tend to pull one head at a time from the crock, as needed, and store the remaining heads at room temperature, in the crock. I revel in the flavor and texture differences that happen over time.

Soak the napa cabbage or rinse thoroughly in cool water to remove any dirt or debris trapped within its leaves. Pack the cabbages into very large bowls or hotel pans. Mix the salt into 4 quarts (3.8 L) of the water and stir until the salt is dissolved. Pour the brine over the cabbages and top them with a plate to keep them under the brine. Allow to soak for 48 hours until the heads are limp and heavy.

After soaking, thoroughly drain the cabbage, being careful to support the heads so that they do not break apart. Pat them dry. Wet heads of napa cabbage will result in a very wet, brined kimchi.

In a saucepan, heat 2 cups (470 ml) of the water over medium-high heat. Whisk the rice flour into the remaining 1 cup (235 ml) water until relatively smooth. When the water in the pan reaches a boil, pour the rice slurry in, whisking constantly. Reduce the heat to medium and continue whisking until the mixture thickens, about 1 minute. Remove from the heat and move to the refrigerator to cool to room temperature and thicken further.

Julienne the daikon and place in a bowl. Chop the chives into 2-inch (5 cm) long pieces and add them to the bowl with the daikon. Coarsely chop the unpeeled ginger and the peeled garlic and onions and place into the bowl of a food processor along with the fish sauce, shrimp, and gochugaru and the cooled rice mixture. You may need to work in batches, depending on the size of your food processor. Blend into a smooth paste, scraping down the sides as necessary.

Put on your kimchi gloves. Thoroughly mix all but 1 cup (225 g) of the spice paste in with the daikon and chives.

Hold the base of a head of cabbage in your nondominant hand and allow the leaves to fall open to the sides like a flower. Gently push apart the center of the core and rub the daikon mix all over the inside and outsides of the leaves. Continue doing this with each layer of cabbage leaves, closing them back up once there is a bit of mix in there. This will add some bulk to your softened head of cabbage. Repeat with each head. Before placing each head into the crock, use your hand to slather a bit of the reserved 1 cup (225 g) of spice paste over the exterior cabbage leaves.

Carefully place each cabbage head flat into the crock. Work carefully to fit the heads together until they are mostly flat packed, keeping as much of the vegetable mix packed inside as possible. Scrape the remaining spice paste and daikon mix out of the bowl and spread it over the top of the layered cabbages. Apply the weight and cover the crock. More liquid will release from the cabbages and they will submerge.

Ferment for 1 to 2 weeks at room temperature. This is one you can definitely eat from the crock. Always remove kimchi with clean hands and utensils.

Yield: 6 to 8 heads of kimchi

The amount of brine needed will vary based on the size of the cabbages and the size of the vessel you choose for brining. Use a concentration of 2 teaspoons (14 g) kosher salt per 1 cup (235 ml) filtered water for a 6% brine.

Ingredients

*Per gallon (3.8 L)
of crock space:*

10 **thin cobs of corn,
shucked and rinsed**

5 **tablespoons (90 g)
kosher salt**

10 **cups (2.4 L)
filtered water**

CORN ON THE COB

Some call these sweet and sour corncobs because some of the corn sweetness remains after fermentation, but the distinctive sour flavors of fermentation are also prominent. The best thing about these cobs is that you can eat them straight from the crock, uncooked, on a hot summer night.

Rinse the cobs, removing any remaining silk. Stand whole cobs on end in the crock. They should fit closely together, with 3 to 4 inches (7.5 to 10 cm) of space at the top of the crock. Stir the salt into the water until dissolved and then pour the brine over the cobs until they are just covered. Place weights on corn and cover crock. Allow to ferment for 1 to 2 weeks. The corn will be more sour and less sweet at 2 weeks.

The cobs will keep in the fridge for a week or more.

Yield: 10 cobs of corn

RECIPE NOTE

The amount of brine may vary based on the size of your corncobs. Use a concentration of 1 tablespoon (18 g) kosher salt per 2 cups (470 ml) filtered water for a 4% brine.

Ingredients

Per 3 gallons (11.4 L)
of crock space:

- 5 heads red cabbage (about 13 pounds, or 6 kg)
- 1 bulb of garlic, peeled
- ¼ cup (27 g) caraway seeds
- 1 bunch of dill
- 1 red onion, thickly sliced
- 8 small, dried Thai chile peppers (optional)
- 5 bay leaves
- 5 juniper berries
- 1⅓ cups (245 g) kosher salt
- 1½ gallons (5.7 L) filtered water

SAUERKRAUT STEAK

In a Polish and Ukrainian-rooted American family, it's pretty likely that you have some serious cabbage traditions. In my family, it's gwumpki (also called stuffed cabbage). If my dad didn't keep to his pre–Christmas Eve tradition of boiling cabbage and rolling gwumpki until 2 or 3 a.m., I don't think my family would recognize the next night as Christmas Eve. In my pickle-related efforts to reconnect to my heritage, I've come across *so* many ways of pickling cabbage. I've probably tasted hundreds of versions before making this one my new cabbage tradition. I love to imagine my own ancestors popping a crock of this open during the cold, gray, Ukrainian winter to discover the brightest burst of color and flavor.

Rinse the cabbages and remove and set aside any undesirable outer leaves. Cut the cabbages in half.

Place the garlic, caraway, dill, onion, chiles, bay leaves, and juniper berries into the crock and begin the process of fitting in the cabbage halves. Don't be afraid to maneuver. Leave 4 inches (10 cm) at the top of the crock. If you can't get the halves to fit, or if they're just a bit too high in the crock, remove 1 or 2 halves and cut them in half. Cabbage quarters can be fit in a bit more easily than halves. Apply the crock weights.

Stir the salt into the water until dissolved and then pour the brine into the crock until there is a 1-inch (2.5 cm) brine layer above the cabbage.

Ferment for 2 to 5 months. Serve as thick slices.

Yield: 5 heads of cabbage

This recipe is intended for a 3-gallon (11.4-liter) crock, so you may need more or less brine depending on the size of your cabbage and the shape of your crock. Use a concentration of 2 teaspoons (11 g) kosher salt per 1 cup (235 ml) filtered water for a 4.5% brine.

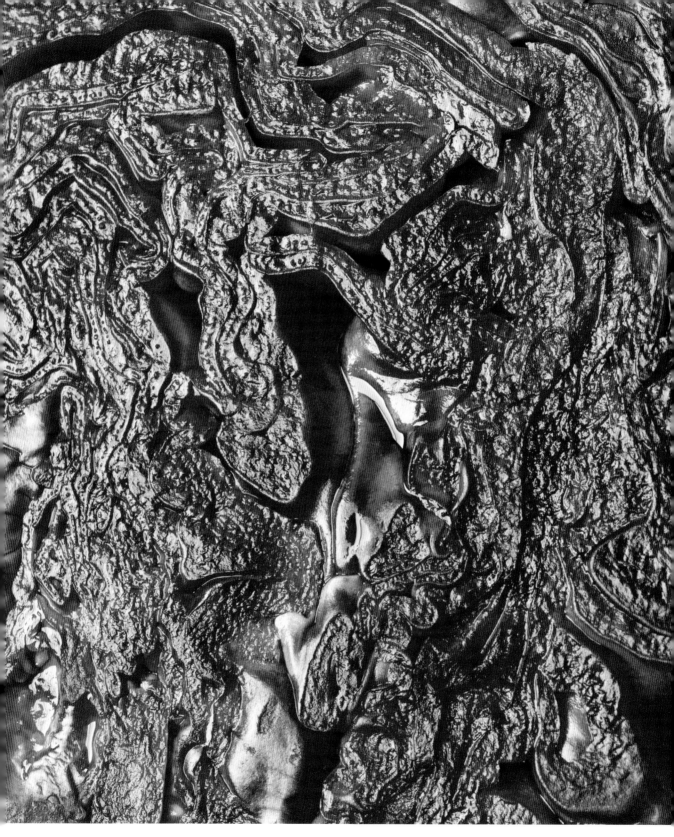

CHAPTER SEVEN

No~Salt~Added Ferments

Throughout this book, you've read about the important role salt plays in vegetable fermentation. But salt isn't actually necessary for safe and successful vegetable fermentation. There are common ferments, both contemporary and traditional, that do not involve the use of any added salt.

There are good reasons to use salt for vegetable fermentation, however. Salt is a powerful preservative, so salted vegetable ferments will last longer. Salt provides the essential elements for a crispy pickle, too. Some dangerous bacteria are halophobic (salt-fearing), while lactic acid bacteria do just fine with even a hearty dose of salt and using even a small amount of salt gives the good guys an advantage over the bad during fermentation. But since it is ultimately the creation of lactic acid and the resulting low pH that makes ferments safe to consume, you can absolutely ferment safely without salt.

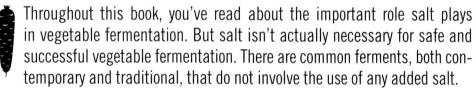

Tips and Guidelines

The techniques detailed here rely on foods and liquids that are naturally high in tannins to keep vegetables crisp, as well as vegetables that are a bit higher in natural salt (but still significantly higher in KCl [potassium] than NaCl [sodium]). Tea, for instance, is high in tannins, while coconut water and Balanced Broth (page 184) are naturally rich in salts. The techniques in this chapter may be applied to other vegetables or other recipes in this book, but harder vegetables (radishes, beets, turnips, carrots, etc.) will be much better choices for no-salt-added fermentation than softer ones (cucumbers, bell peppers, or collard greens).

Using Tea

Tea is rich in tannins, an ingredient that is often used to make softer vegetables stay crispy during fermentation. Since the biggest taste issue with saltless pickles is the lack of crispness, tea definitely makes a great choice. Feel free to use your favorite variety of tea, but for best results, choose a tea that is free of preservatives and maltodextrin. The tea works as both a flavoring agent and a source of tannins to pick up some of the slack that occurs when salt is absent, so have fun trying different teas to match. The Earl Grey Fennel Beets (page 181) in this chapter are a favorite of both salt-free and salt-loving fermenters who've learned from me.

Using Broth

This special homemade broth (Balanced Broth, page 184) is made with vegetables that have a naturally high salt content. It is a natural way to make vegetables extra tasty and a bit less soft than they would be if just fermented in water. The vegetables used are high sodium but much higher in potassium, which has a balancing effect on sodium for those concerned about blood pressure.

Using Coconut Water

Coconut water has been ascribed many miracle, healing powers. I can't speak to those, but I can tell you that it makes a great fermenting liquid. Ferments made with coconut water bubble a lot and have a wonderful, distinctive flavor.

CELERIAC BEET KRAUT

I spent many a month attempting salt-free sauerkraut with very little success. A straight-up pile of mush was the result of almost every trial. Beets and celeriac do the best job of all the elements I've found at keeping kraut crisp, but don't expect the texture of a salted kraut.

½ pound (225 g) cabbage, cut into ¼-inch (5 mm) shreds

¼ cup (60 g) peeled, grated celery root

¼ cup (56 g) thinly sliced, quartered beets

Filtered water, for topping off

Combine the cabbage, celery root, and beets in a large bowl. Squeeze and squeeze until you see some juice appear. You will not see puddles of liquid as you do with salted sauerkraut, and the texture of the cabbage will not change dramatically.

Pack the vegetables into a pint (500 ml) jar, pressing them down as best you can. Top with filtered water. Using your preferred method (see pages 23 to 28), weight the vegetables down and cover your jar.

Ferment for 1 week or longer if they're still crisp at that point. Remove the weight, secure the lid, and place the jar in the fridge. This doesn't stay crisp very long, so plan to eat it within a couple of weeks. If it gets too soft, purée and enjoy as a spread or dip.

Yield: 1 pint (450 g)

WHITE BEAN SAUERKRAUT DIP

One of the downsides to salt-free kraut is the texture. It just doesn't get that crisp. I've always been one for looking on the bright side, so my trick for soft kraut is to find a dish where soft is desirable. Enter this dip. Between the acid from the kraut and the generous use of herbs, you won't miss the salt one bit.

¾ cup (180 g) Celeriac Beet Kraut or your favorite salt-free sauerkraut

½ cup (90 g) fresh cooked or (131 g) canned, salt-free cannellini beans

1½ teaspoons (1 g) dried sage leaves

½ teaspoon (0.5 g) dried thyme

Drain the sauerkraut well and rinse and drain the beans. Put all the ingredients in the food processor and process until smooth, about 3 minutes.

Yield: 1 cup (300 g)

RECIPE NOTES

• If you eat salt, feel free to try this with a salty sauerkraut!

• Serve with pita chips or crudités.

Ingredients

- 14 ounces (390 g) burdock root
- 2 ounces (55 g) turmeric root
- 2 cups (470 ml) coconut water

HEALING BURDOCK TURMERIC PICKLES

I have suffered from eczema since the day I was born. The doctor actually told my mom in the delivery room that I would never have acne because of it, which just goes to show how poorly autoimmune issues were understood at the time! I still do get occasional flare-ups, and when I do, I like to have a bit of this anti-inflammatory pickle on hand to help me out. Burdock is believed to help specifically with eczema, and turmeric is an all-purpose good guy for your anti-inflammatory needs. Combined, they taste great and give aid.

Cut the burdock and turmeric roots into ¼-inch (5 mm) thick coins. Place both in a quart (1 L) jar and pour the coconut water over until they are just covered. Using your preferred method (see pages 23 to 28), weight the vegetables down and cover your jar. Coconut water ferments tend to bubble vigorously, so leave at least an inch (2.5 cm) of space between the surface of the liquid and the rim of the jar and keep your jar stored on a plate or an old kitchen towel during fermentation.

Ferment for 5 days to 2 weeks. Remove the weight, secure the lid, and place the jar in the fridge.

Yield: 1 quart (900 g)

RECIPE NOTE — Turmeric stains are virtually impossible to get out (just ask my wood countertops), so be sure to put turmeric straight in the jar and avoid touching anything else until you've washed your hands.

SPICED GREEN BEANS

Coconut water ferments are loads of fun. They bubble a lot, and they have a distinctive flavor that can definitely be habit-forming. Like the other salt-free methods found in this chapter, using coconut water to ferment doesn't feel like a compromise, but like a new, fermenty adventure. Coconut water ferments will definitely end up a bit more sour than brine ferments.

1 inch (2.5 cm) of ginger, unpeeled and sliced

1 cinnamon stick

1 allspice berry

½ teaspoon (0.5 g) red pepper flakes

½ pound (225 g) green beans, ends trimmed

1 cup (235 ml) coconut water

Place all the spices in a pint (500 ml) jar. Gently fill the jar with green beans. Don't pack them too tightly, as bruised beans make for soft pickles. The beans should reach about 1 inch (2.5 cm) below the rim of the jar. Pour the coconut water over the beans until they are just covered.

Using your preferred method (see pages 23 to 28), weight the vegetables down and cover your jar. Coconut water ferments tend to bubble vigorously, so keep your jar on a plate or an old kitchen towel during fermentation.

Ferment at room temperature for 5 to 10 days. By 10 days, the green beans will be softening a bit.

Yield: 1 pint (450 g)

EARL GREY FENNEL BEETS

When it comes to tea, I used to be very boring. I loved the citrusy tang of Earl Grey, and I would drink almost nothing else. Then I became friends with tea expert Alexis Siemons, who opened my eyes to the many shades of tea that I'd been missing. I still love Earl Grey, though, so I took inspiration from Alexis and started cooking with it.

1 beet (½ pound, or 225 g), trimmed, greens removed

1 ounce (28 g) thinly sliced fennel bulb

¾ cup (180 ml) cold-brewed Earl Grey tea (page 182)

Slice the unpeeled beets into ½-inch (1.5 cm) slices and place in a pint (500 ml) jar (cut the slices in half, if necessary, to fit them in). Slide the pieces of fennel bulb in around the sides. Pour the tea over the beets until they are just covered, leaving 1 inch (2.5 cm) of space at the top of the jar. Using your preferred method (see pages 23 to 28), weight the vegetables down and cover your jar.

Ferment for 1 week or longer if they're still crisp at that point. Remove the weight, secure the lid, and place the jar in the fridge. These don't last as long as salted pickles, so plan to eat within a couple of weeks.

Yield: 1 pint (450 g)

TANNIN TEA

A few years back, I finally realized that cold brewing tea was the way to a perfect summer cup. Never heating the tea leaves means never taking a bitter sip. The flavors of the tea dominate the bitter notes, and this has made me a lifelong convert. Brewing cold is a simple process that requires a bit more tea than brewing hot.

1 quart (940 ml) filtered water, at room temperature

5 tea bags or 4 teaspoons (8 g) loose green or black tea, any variety

Pour the water into a quart (1 L) jar and add the tea. Close the jar and allow to soak at room temperature or in the fridge for 8 to 12 hours and up to 24 hours.

Remove the tea bags or strain out the loose tea.

Store the tea in the fridge and bring back to room temperature before using for fermentation. Use within a week.

Yield: 1 quart (1 L)

SENCHA DAIKON PICKLES ››

A lovely Japanese green tea paired with a lovely Japanese radish is all it takes to make this simple, crispy, and delicately flavored pickle. The flavor of the tea here is quite subtle, and the cold-brewing process ensures that there is no bitterness. These pickles are very sour, but also very fresh and clean tasting. Serve alongside a bowl of warming miso soup.

1 small daikon (½ pound, or 225 g)

¾ cup (175 ml) cold-brewed sencha green tea

Trim the daikon and cut into strips that are ½ inch (1.5 cm) wide and 3 to 4 inches (7.5 to 10 cm) long. Stand them on end in a pint (500 ml) jar and pour the tea over the top until the daikon is covered and there is about 1 inch (2.5 cm) of space between the brine and the rim of the jar. Using your preferred method (see pages 23 to 28), weight the vegetables down and cover your jar.

Ferment at room temperature for 5 to 7 days. Remove the weight, secure the lid, and place the jar in the fridge.

Yield: 1 pint (450 g)

BALANCED BROTH

My friend Beth has never loved to cook, but she did introduce me to the concept of drinking broth. It's a simple recipe, and it's savory, warming, and healthful to have on hand in the colder months. The version of the broth I make has a great, natural balance of potassium and sodium, which makes it ideal for salt-free fermenting.

6 carrots

3 beets, trimmed

1 small celery root, peeled

1 small leek, chopped and soaked to remove grit

1 bunch of celery, leaves on

3 quarts (3 L) filtered water

Wash and chop all the vegetables into large chunks and place them in a 6-quart (6 L) pot. Pour the water into the pot and bring to a boil over high heat. Cover, reduce the heat, and allow to simmer for 1 hour. Transfer to the fridge to cool before using for fermentation. You can make this up to 5 days in advance.

Yield: 3 quarts (3 L)

BROTH-PICKLED KOHLRABI ››

Kohlrabi looks like a creature from a faraway planet, but its flavor and texture are so familiar. Its brassica cousins include other wonderful fermenters like cabbage and cauliflower. Along with radishes, turnips, rutabaga, and beets, it makes a great option for broth pickles because it has a texture that stays crispy, even without an overabundance of salt.

1 kohlrabi root, trimmed and washed

1 cup (235 ml) Balanced Broth

Chop the kohlrabi into ¼- to ½-inch (5 mm to 1.5 cm) sticks. Pack the pieces into a pint (500 ml) jar and add the broth until the kohlrabi is just covered. There should be about 1 inch (2.5 cm) of headspace at the top of the jar. Using your preferred method (see pages 23 to 28), weight the vegetables down and cover your jar.

Ferment for 7 to 10 days or longer if they're still crisp at that point. Remove the weight, secure the lid, and place the jar in the fridge.

Yield: 1 pint (450 g)

Safely Salt-Free

The tricks to excellent salt-free ferments are to pay close attention to smell and appearance and to find a reliable way to test pH. Problems that *very* seldom occur in salted vegetable ferments do occur more frequently in salt-free fermentation. Off smells, reminiscent of cheese (especially Swiss cheese) and rotten eggs should be taken very seriously. They could indicate an unwanted secondary fermentation, and batches with those smells should be discarded and not tasted. Salt-free batches are more prone to colorful molds, and those batches should also be discarded. The safest bet in salt-free fermentation is to use a pH meter to test the acidity of the finished product before you eat it. If the pH reads below 4.0 on a pH meter or test strip, the ferment is safe to eat.

For many people, it seems that the actual issue with salt is the large amount hidden in highly processed foods, and that a bit of salt added to homemade foods, like pickles or kraut, isn't really a problem. But if you have decided to eliminate dietary salt for whatever reason, these recipes are for you. Even if you don't avoid salt, the methods outlined in this section make great-tasting pickles that everyone can enjoy.

CHAPTER EIGHT

Tsukemono, Sun Pickles, and Other Paths to Cultured Vegetables

The recipes in this chapter offer entirely different ways to ferment and culture vegetables. Few of the methods used for in part two will be relevant when you're building culturing beds, like the misodoko or nukadoko. Likewise, yeast fermentation/Garlic Honey (page 194) has totally different rules than bacterial fermentation. And the all-important submersion? It's not required when making Hari Mirch Achaar (page 197).

Each type of fermentation touched upon here rightly boasts a bevy of books and articles devoted to it alone. This goal of this chapter is to offer you a way to look through the telescope and discover a few little corners of the fermentation universe that may lead you to deeper exploration.

Culturing and Making "Quick" Japanese Pickles

The Japanese pickling tradition, which has a rich history and involves many different styles (many of which do not involve fermentation), is as close as we, the fermenters, get to "quick pickles." Let me be clear—the pickling itself is quick but the methods we're covering here involve making a bed for your pickles to lie in. The building of the bed is the key (especially for Nukadoko, page 191), and that sometimes requires care that goes well beyond what needs to be done for the simple pickles in earlier chapters, but the results are wonderfully unique.

Ingredients

- 1 cup (250 g) miso
- ¼ cup (60 ml) mirin
- 3 cloves of garlic, finely minced
- 1 inch (2.5 cm) of ginger, peeled and finely minced
- A few fine grinds of pepper

BUILDING A MISODOKO

Making miso-cultured pickles (misozuke) is extremely easy and the process is quick by anyone's standards (not just a fermenter's). Any flavors you add to the pickling bed will be absorbed into the pickles, so keep that in mind if culturing onions, garlic, or hot peppers. These pickles, like many tsukemono, are extremely salty, so I like them best paired with lightly seasoned dishes or grains.

In a small bowl, combine all the ingredients. Pack into a 2- to 3-cup (475 to 710 ml), food-safe, glass container with a tight-fitting lid and then add the vegetables (see Recipe Notes for details).

For best results, store in the refrigerator when not in use or when culturing for longer periods.

Yield: 2 to 3 cups (450 to 680 g)

RECIPE NOTES

- Vegetable options are basically unlimited. If you use vegetables with a higher water content, you will "age" your bed more quickly, meaning that it won't be around for as many batches, but a misodoko is easy to make, and cucumber, bell peppers, and leaves of all sorts are fun misozuke, so try them all!

- White miso is fermented for the shortest time of the common misos, so it will be the least salty and the sweetest. Red miso will be the most flavorful and saltiest option. Experiment to find your favorite combination.

- This can be a very long or short process. I've aged some vegetables (Miso Sunchokes, page 190) for longer than 6 months and done others for as little as an hour or two. Shorter periods yield slightly salty and lightly flavored vegetables, while longer periods result in vegetables that are dramatically altered in color and texture. There's no reason not to taste a piece or two every day to see where your preferences lie.

- It's okay to peel your vegetables! The microbes that will be culturing your vegetables come from the miso, not from the vegetables, which means you're free to remove the peel of any vegetable you put into the bed.

- Rinsing after removing the vegetables from the bed is traditional but not required. It will remove any extra miso bits and make the pickles slightly less salty.

- Over time and several batches, the bed will get watery from all the vegetables you're putting in. Once it is truly wet, much of the flavor will be gone, so it may be time to a make a new bed and to add that misodoko to a giant batch of soup.

- Once you've removed your vegetables, either reuse your miso bed immediately with fresh vegetables or cover and put it in the refrigerator until you're ready to use it again.

MISO RHUBARB

I especially enjoy high acid vegetables pickled in miso. The saltiness of the miso is balanced by the acidity of the rhubarb, and the rhubarb itself is transformed and barely recognizable after even a few days in the misodoko. Vegetables shrink significantly during their culturing period due to the high salt content of miso, so it can be tricky to fish them all out of their comfy pickling place. In her excellent book *Asian Pickles*, Karen Solomon recommends using cheesecloth to avoid losing any savory bites. I don't mind digging to find the occasional, extra-aged surprise, but Solomon's method does reduce the amount of miso bed lost during the removal of the vegetables.

1 misodoko (page 189)

2 stalks of rhubarb, chopped into 1-inch (2.5 cm) pieces

Place half of your miso mixture into the container and top with a layer of cheesecloth. Place the rhubarb on the cheesecloth and then place another layer of cheesecloth on the vegetables. Pack the remaining miso mixture on top of the top cheesecloth, allowing the ends of the cloth to protrude from the container for easy lifting. Pack the miso down with a wooden spoon and put the lid on the container. Move to the refrigerator or leave at room temperature.

Allow to culture for 1 week. Pull up the sides of the cheesecloth to reveal the cultured rhubarb beneath. Dice and use as a salty, tangy seasoning.

Yield: ¾ cup (170 g)

MISO SUNCHOKES

Sunchokes are one of my favorite vegetables to put into the miso bed for several reasons. First, I can be a little lazy with my bed, and sometimes I miss a vegetable or two when I'm digging through with my fork. With sunchokes, it doesn't matter at all. I've had a stray slice sit in the bed in the back of the fridge for months and months and when I finally dug it out, it was perfectly crispy, salty, and ready to be eaten. There is also something so unexpectedly lovely about the complex umami of the miso bed and the light artichoke flavor of the sunchoke.

½ cup (75 g) sliced sunchoke

1 misodoko (page 189)

Bury the sunchoke slices in the miso bed. Press down a bit to pack the bed. (Or use Karen Soloman's miso method outlined in the Miso Rhubarb recipe). Cover the container and move to the fridge. Allow to ferment for 1 to 6 months. The sunchoke should be crisp but almost translucent, like a water chestnut. Rinse and enjoy.

Yield: ½ cup (115 g)

Ingredients

- 1 pound (450 g) rice bran
- 4 pieces of kombu, cut into small strips
- 2 cloves of garlic, minced
- 1 inch (2.5 cm) of ginger, minced
- 1 tablespoon (9 g) mustard powder
- 1 teaspoon (1 g) red pepper flakes
- 1¼ cups (300 ml) filtered water
- ½ cup (120 ml) beer
- ½ cup (150 g) fine salt
- 1 cup (150 g) vegetables scraps per week

BUILDING A NUKADOKO

Every nukadoko seems to have its own signature flavors. Some are more sour than others, and some are smoky or meaty. Even in my own home, I've never built two that produce the same flavors. Even if your lifestyle won't allow for the necessary long-term maintenance, try making one and maintaining it as long as you can. These pickles are worth the work. Feeding the bed vegetable scraps inoculates it with lactic acid bacteria and hints of flavor.

In your largest skillet and working in batches, toast the rice bran over medium heat, making sure the bran layer is no more than ¾ inch (2 cm) deep. Stir constantly until it darkens slightly and becomes very fragrant, like freshly baked cookies, about 2 minutes. If it starts to smell like popcorn, remove from heat, stir vigorously, and turn the heat down a bit. Let it cool.

In a ½-gallon (2 L) or slightly larger container, stir together the cooled rice bran, kombu, garlic, ginger, mustard powder, and red pepper flakes, distributing the seasonings throughout the bran.

Combine the water, beer, and salt and stir until salt is dissolved. Pour the liquid into the rice bran. Stir until a thick paste forms. If the bed is too dry to stir with reasonable ease, add more water, 1 tablespoon (15 ml) at a time, until the mixture is just flexible enough to allow you to easily bury and find vegetable pieces.

Add vegetable scraps into the bed and stir to distribute. Stir your bed daily. Once a week, remove as many vegetable scraps as possible and discard them, returning back as much rice bran mixture from the scraps as you can. Due to the high salt content of the bed, the vegetable scraps will shrink significantly during this priming period. Once you've removed them, add a fresh batch of vegetable scraps. Repeat for 4 to 6 weeks until the smell of the bed is pleasantly sour. See Nuka-Cukes and Radishes (page 192) for proceeding with making pickles.

Although you'll be returning as much bran mixture as possible to your vessel, each time you remove pickles, you'll be losing a little bit of volume, as well as salt and flavor that are, as intended, sucked into the vegetables. With daily use, you may need to replenish the bed by adding salt, toasted bran, water, and seasonings as frequently as once a month.

Yield: ½ gallon (1.9 L)

Good candidates for vegetable scraps include turnip and radish peels and the hard outer leaves and cores of cauliflower, broccoli, and cabbage. Avoid members of the onion family, since larger amounts will impart too much flavor, and be aware that carrots and beets can leach color into the bed.

Ingredients

1 **English cucumber**

1 **bunch of radishes, greens removed**

1 **nukadoko (page 191)**

NUKA CUKES AND RADISHES

Once you've established your nuka-bed, the hard part is over. The process of actually making nukazuke (nuka pickles) is simple and very flexible. Just about any vegetable will work, but nuka cukes are particular favorites. For a quick pickle, I slice them on the bias into 1-inch chunks and let them culture for an hour to a day. When I'm feeling more patient, I push them in whole, add a bunch of radishes, and wait a week, as outlined below.

With very clean hands, push the cucumber and radishes into the nukadoko until they are fully submerged and lightly press down on the top of the rice bran to make sure the vegetables are all packed in.

After 5 to 7 days, remove the (now wilted) vegetables and scrape any remaining rice bran mixture back into the bed. Use the pickles within a few hours.

Stir the empty bed and add fresh vegetables for pickling. If you don't want to start the pickling process again immediately, be sure to stir the empty bed at least once a day until you add fresh vegetables.

Yield: 1 to 2 cups (225 to 450 g)

Ingredients

5 bulbs of garlic, peeled and separated into cloves

10 ounces (280 g) raw honey

GARLIC HONEY

When I was a kid, my mom skipped the cough syrup in favor of a homemade remedy of honey, a drop or two of whiskey, and lemon. I'm sure this mixture would be frowned upon today, but it was tasty and it did calm my nighttime coughs. This recipe, adapted from Ikuko Hisamatsu's book *Quick & Easy Tsukemono*, is my answer to my mom's old remedy. This is a long ferment and the only yeast ferment in this book.

Place the garlic cloves in a pint (500 ml) jar, filling to 1½ inches (4 cm) below the rim, and add the honey. Some raw honey is more solid than liquid, so you may need to add small amounts and allow it time to seep into the jar before adding more. Stir and cover with lid. Stir daily for a few weeks to submerge garlic and stir in any honey deposits at the bottom of the jar before adding more. As fermentation progresses, the honey will bubble and the garlic will release its water, making the honey more liquid and the cloves shrunken and brown. Once the contents are in this state, reduce stirring to every 3 to 4 days.

After 3 months of fermentation, you may start to take 1 tablespoon (15 g) of honey or a clove of garlic, as needed, as a curative. Store in the refrigerator.

Yield: 1 pint (500 ml)

RECIPE NOTE

This recipe is essentially a kind of garlic mead, which means it is not made for its probiotics. Getting the pH low enough and the alcohol high enough for optimal safety will take quite a bit longer than it does in lactic acid fermentation. This recipe should ideally be pH tested before consuming. Once the pH has reached safe levels (4.0 or below), move to the fridge for storage.

Garlic Honey at 4 days (left)
and 3 months (right).

Indian Sun Pickles

Understanding why these pickles work requires understanding a few specifics of vegetable fermentation. Lactic acid bacteria are facultative anaerobes, which means that they generally do their converting work in an oxygen-free environment, but they can switch gears and keep on truckin' if oxygen is present.

Because of the unorthodox methodology used to make these pickles, you should not vary salt or lemon juice levels as you would in other recipes. Rest assured that there is a long tradition of this kind of pickle in India, in the hot sun, and you can always measure pH to be safe.

Note that these aren't the easiest pickles to make. They require several steps and a bit of attention, but they keep in the fridge for a good long while (a year or more) and their flavors make them well worth the extra bit of effort. If the flavors get too hot or intense, try blending a small amount and using it as a spread for idli, dosai, or any other fermented Indian bread.

Ingredients

- ½ cup (88 g) mustard seeds
- ½ teaspoon (1 g) nigella seeds or black cumin (shah jeera) seeds
- 5 whole black peppercorns
- ½ teaspoon (1 g) fennel seeds
- 1 teaspoon (3 g) fenugreek seeds
- 1½ tablespoons (27 g) kosher salt
- 1 tablespoon (7 g) turmeric powder
- 1 pound (450 g) chili peppers (about 50), washed, caps removed, and chopped into 1-inch (2.5 cm) pieces
- 5 tablespoons (75 ml) fresh lemon juice
- 1 cup (235 ml) mustard oil

HARI MIRCH ACHAAR (INDIAN HOT PEPPER PICKLE)

If you can't find the slender, green Hari Mirch peppers, cayenne or any other slim and spicy pepper will do the trick. These pickles are traditionally made in the summer when bright sunshine will heat things up fast, but I sometimes cheat and do them in my kitchen, completely indoors.

Grind the whole seed spices into powder in a spice grinder and combine with the salt and turmeric powder.

Place the pepper pieces into a quart (1 L) jar and add the spice powder. Mix thoroughly or put a lid on it and shake to distribute the spice powder. Press the peppers back down so they are mostly covered in the spice powder.

Place the lid on the jar, but leave it just loose enough to let CO_2 escape. Place your jar outside in a sunny spot. Bring it in at night and put it back out the next morning. Repeat for a total of 3 days, stirring thoroughly each night when you bring it in.

The night of the third day, add the lemon juice. Stir or shake very well.

Put it back outside for 2 more days, bring it in, and shake/stir well each night.

At the end of the last night, bring your sun pickle inside for good. Heat the mustard oil in a saucepan over high heat for 5 minutes, until smoking. Remove from the heat, let it cool to room temperature, and then pour over your veggie/spice mix. Stir well. Use a spatula or spoon to scrape excess spice mixture from the sides down into the jar.

Let it sit overnight, inside at room temperature, and start tasting 3 days later. The oil shouldn't smell "oily" when these are ready to eat; it should be infused with the flavors of the spices and peppers. It may up to a week for the flavors to fully infuse.

Once they're infused, store in the refrigerator.

Yield: 1 quart (900 g)

Heating the mustard oil can cause coughing. Open windows, turn on the vent fan, and be prepared to leave the kitchen if you feel your throat tickle or your eyes water.

Ingredients

- 1 tablespoon (6 g) cardamom seeds
- 2 tablespoons (12 g) cumin seeds
- 1 tablespoon (5 g) black peppercorns
- 1 tablespoon (11 g) mustard seeds
- 1½ tablespoons (27 g) kosher salt
- 2 cups (244 g) 1-inch (2.5 cm) carrot pieces (4 to 5 carrots)
- 3 tablespoons (45 ml) fresh lemon juice
- 1 tablespoon (8 g) turmeric powder
- 1 cup (235 ml) mustard oil

CARROT CARDAMOM SUN PICKLE

This is for the cardamom lovers. Unlike with the simple lacto pickles in earlier chapters that I eat by the handful, I reserve these pickles exclusively for seasoning. The spices are intense and they keep for a long time in the fridge, so I love puréeing small amounts of this pickle and throwing it in the pan to cook with onions or cauliflower.

Grind the whole spices into a powder in a coffee or spice grinder and mix thoroughly with the salt.

Place the carrots into a quart (1 L) jar and add the powdered spices. Place a lid on the jar and shake well. Push the carrots down so that they are covered in spices.

Replace the lid, but leave it loose enough to let CO_2 escape, and place your jar outside in a sunny spot. Bring it inside at night and put it back out the next morning. Repeat for a total of 3 days, stirring thoroughly each night when you bring it in.

The night of the third day, add the fresh lemon juice and turmeric powder. Stir or shake very well.

Put it back outside for 2 more days, bring it in, and shake/stir well each night.

At the end of the second night, bring your sun pickle inside for good. Heat the mustard oil in a saucepan over high heat for approximately 5 minutes. Remove from the heat, let it cool to room temperature, and pour over your veggie/spice mix. Stir well.

Let it sit overnight, inside, at room temperature and start tasting 1 day later. The oil shouldn't smell "oily" when these are ready to eat; it should be infused with the flavors of the spices. It may take up to 3 days on the counter to fully infuse.

Once they're ready, use a spatula or spoon to scrape excess spice mixture from the sides down into the jar and stir again. Store in the refrigerator.

Yield: 1 quart (900 g)

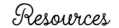

Ingredients

Amazon
www.amazon.com
Rice bran (do not buy "stabilized"),
spices, specialty ingredients

H-Mart
www.hmart.com
Gochugaru, other
kimchi ingredients

Kalustyan's
www.kalustyans.com
Spices, mustard oil

Mountain Rose Herbs
www.mountainroseherbs.com
Spices

PureFormulas
www.pureformulas.com
Rice bran (do not buy "stabilized")

World Spice Merchants
www.worldspice.com
Spices and spice blends

Vessels and Equipment

Fante's
www.fantes.com
Fido and LeParfait, European-
style, gasket-sealing jars in
a variety of sizes

Fillmore Container
www.fillmorecontainer.com
Jars of all sorts and reCAP lids

Midwest Supplies
www.midwestsupplies.com
PH strips, airlocks and bungs,
food-grade plastic buckets

Miki Palchick
www.mikipalchick.com
Handmade water-sealing crocks

Ogusky Ceramics
www.claycrocks.com
Handcrafted, open crocks

Ohio Stoneware
www.ohiocaststone.com
Open crocks in a wide
variety of sizes

Pottery by Sandy Der
*www.etsy.com/shop/
PotteryBySandyDer*
Pickling weights

Sarah Kersten
sarahkersten.com/fermentationjar
Handmade, water-sealing,
1½-gallon (5.7 L) crocks

Stone Creek Trading
www. stonecreektrading.com
European water-sealing crocks in
a variety of sizes, kraut shredders
and pounders

Tamarack Stoneware
*www.etsy.com/shop/Tamarack
Stoneware*
Pickling weights

Fermentation Information
(see "Bibliography" for
further reading)

**Cultures for Health Blog
and Newsletter**
blog.culturesforhealth.com

Nordic Food Lab
www.nordicfoodlab.org

Phickle (my website)
www.phickle.com

Pickle Bibliography
*fbns.ncsu.edu/USDAARS/html/
Fflbiblio1.htm*

Wild Fermentation
www.wildfermentation.com

Appendix

Salt Chart

How you salt your ferments is a matter of taste. Weighing is more accurate, but of course, your salt preferences may change from one vegetable to the next, and all salts are not equally salty.

A range somewhere between 2 and 5 percent salt by weight is generally used for directly salting vegetables, and a range of 4 to 6 percent is common for salt brines. In practice, the range for direct salting can vary widely, from no salt at all to 8 percent (inedible, by most standards) for cases where preservation is a matter of survival over taste.

APPROXIMATE WEIGHTS/VOLUME EQUIVALENTS OF DIFFERENT SALT TYPES

Measurement	Fine (Table) (g)	Fine (Higher Mineral) (g)	Coarse (g)	Kosher (g)	Rock (g)	Flake (g)
1 teaspoon	5 to 6	7 to 8	6 to 7	6 to 7	7 to 8	3 to 4
1 tablespoon	16 to 17	21 to 23	17 to 20	17 to 19	21 to 23	12 to 13

APPROXIMATE DIRECT SALT PERCENTAGE BY VOLUME AND WEIGHT

Weight of Vegetable	2 percent	2.5 percent	3 percent	4 percent	5 percent
1 pound	1 to 2 teaspoons (9 g)	1½ to 2 teaspoons (11 g)	2 teaspoons (13.5 g)	1 tablespoon (18 g)	4 teaspoons (22 g)
1 kilogram	20 g	25 g	30 g	40 g	50 g

Multiply the gram weight of your vegetable by the percentage you want.
So 450 g (1 pound) of cabbage at 2 percent would be 450 x 0.02 = 9 g salt.

APPROXIMATE BRINE SALT PERCENTAGE BY VOLUME AND WEIGHT

Water	4 percent	5 percent	6 percent	7 percent
1 cup (235 ml)	1 to 2 teaspoons (9 g)	1½ to 2 teaspoons (12 g)	2 teaspoons (14 g)	1 tablespoon (16 g)
1 liter	20 g	25 g	30 g	40 g

Multiply milliliters of water by the brine percentage you want.
So 235 ml (1 cup) of water at 4 percent would be 235 x 0.04 = 9 g salt.

Bibliography

Andoh, Elizabeth, and Leigh Beisch. *Kansha: Celebrating Japan's Vegan & Vegetarian Traditions*. Berkeley, CA: Ten Speed Press, 2010.

Breidt, F., R. F. McFeeters, I. M. Pérez-Díaz, and C. Lee. "Fermented Vegetables." In *Food Microbiology: Fundamentals and Frontiers*, 4th ed., edited by M. P. Doyle and R. L. Buchanan, 841–55. Washington, DC: ASM Press, 2013.

Breidt, F., E. Medina-Pradas, D. Wafa, et al. "Characterization of Cucumber Fermentation Spoilage Bacteria by Enrichment Culture and 16S rDNA Cloning." *Journal of Food Science* 78, no. 3 (2013): M470–76.

Byers, Branden. *The Everyday Fermentation Handbook: A Real-Life Guide to Fermenting Food—Without Losing Your Mind or Your Microbes*. Cincinnati, OH: F + W Media, 2014.

Chun, Lauryn, and Olga Massov. *The Kimchi Cookbook: 60 Traditional and Modern Ways to Make and Eat Kimchi*. Berkeley, CA: Ten Speed Press, 2012.

Etchells, J. L. "Incidence of Yeasts in Cucumber Fermentations." *Food Research* 6, no. 1 (1941): 95–104.

Hisamatsu, Ikuko. *Quick & Easy Tsukemono: Japanese Pickling Recipes*.Tokyo: Japan Publications Trading Co., Inc, 2005.

Johanningsmeier, S. D., and R. F. McFeeters. "Metabolism of Lactic Acid in Fermented Cucumbers by *Lactobacillus buchneri* and Related Species: Potential Spoilage Organisms in Reduced Salt Fermentations." *Food Microbiology* 35, no. 2 (2013): 129–35.

Katz, Sandor Ellix. *The Art of Fermentation: An In-Depth Exploration of Essential Concepts and Processes from around the World*. White River Junction, VT: Chelsea Green Publishing, 2012.

Katz, Sandor Ellix. *Wild Fermentation: The Flavor, Nutrition, and Craft of Live-Culture Foods*. White River Junction, VT: Chelsea Green Publishing, 2003.

Lewin, Alex. *Real Food Fermentation: Preserving Whole Fresh Food with Live Cultures in Your Home Kitchen*. Beverly, MA: Quarry Books, 2012.

Moyer, Melinda Wenner. "It's Time to End the War on Salt." *Scientific American*. July 8, 2011. www.scientificamerican.com/article/its-time-to-end-the-war-on-salt

Rao, M. S., J. Pintado, W. F. Stevens, and J. P. Guyot. "Kinetic Growth Parameters of Different Amylolytic and Non-amylolytic Lactobacillus Strains Under Various Salt and pH Conditions." *Bioresource Technology* 94, no. 3 (2004): 331–7.

Solomon, Karen. *Asian Pickles: Sweet, Sour, Salty, Cured, and Fermented Preserves from Japan, Korea, China, India, and Beyond*. Berkeley, CA: Ten Speed Press, 2014.

Veg Recipes of India. Blog. www.vegrecipesofindia.com/green-chilli-pickle-recipe-hari-mirch-ka-achaar

Veldhuis, M. K., J. L. Etchells, I. D. Jones, and O. Veerhoff. "Notes on Cucumber Salting." *The Fruit Products Journal* 20, no. 11 (1941): 341–2.

Vongerichten, Marja. *The Kimchi Chronicles: Korean Cooking for an American Kitchen*. New York: Rodale Books, 2011.

Acknowledgments

It isn't at all melodramatic to say that this book would not have been possible without the help, love, and support of so many. I have no doubt that this thank you list is incomplete. To all who helped, who tested recipes, who learned the basics of fermentation just for me, you have my eternal gratitude. Thank you for stinking up your homes!

To my agent, **Clare Pellino**, I would not have written this book without your encouragement. Thank you for the prodding and support I needed to undertake this project and for your mad negotiation skills.

To my editor, **Amanda Waddell**, thank you so much for the opportunity to write this book! I am so grateful that I had the chance to work with you and for all the thought, care, and effort you put into this book. Your advocacy took this book to the next level.

Renae Haines, the project master of the universe, thank you for wrangling all the details, patiently answering my noob questions, and pulling things together with speed and panache.

Heather Godin, thank you for your art direction, flexibility, and the tireless work that you did to make this book into a visually cohesive and lovely document of these foods.

Karen Levy, thanks for doing the detailed work of copy-editing. No matter how many times I read this manuscript, I would never have caught the many typos, omissions, and wonky bits that you did.

Courtney Apple, I adore the photos you took, and I will always be impressed that you were able to make my fermented foods look both exactly as they did and luminously beautiful. Your photos make this book special.

Barbara Botting, you have an amazing talent. I am so grateful for the wonderful work you did styling these photos. Very few people can make things look effortlessly gorgeous the way you do.

Dr. Fred Breidt, thank you for your patience and for being such a willing and able public servant. Your decades of tireless research are appreciated by me and by so many other fermenters around the globe. For any errors of interpretation, I am sorry. For all the knowledge you imparted, thank you.

To **Carly Dougherty** of Food & Ferments, thank you for being my Philly fermentation compatriot and for giving of your limited entrepreneur's time so freely. I'm so grateful to you and Dave for making a great product that I can proudly tell others to buy.

To **Jeremy Ogusky**, thank you for the time you spent interviewing with me and, of course, for the lovely crock. It will sit in a proud place on my table, and I promise to keep it filled with bubbling things whenever possible. Next stop: Fermentation Nation!

To **Sandor Katz**, for being a perpetual source of inspiration through your teaching and writing.

To **Will Stallwood**, of Cipher Prime, for your extremely helpful feedback. Your eye is unparalleled and your design guidance ultimately helped to make this book beautiful.

To the gentlemen of Flyclops: **Jake**, **Parker**, **Dave**, **Jay**, and **Josh**, your extreme flexibility allowed me the time and energy to complete this book, and I will be forever grateful. Thank you for your interest and involvement and for your valuable feedback throughout the process.

To my Philly food ladies (**Alexis Siemons**, **Allyson Kramer**, **Jolene Hart**, **Joy Manning**, **Marisa McClellan**, **Robin Shreeves**, and **Tenaya Darlington**), thank you so much for your endless support, encouragement, advice, and for calming my fears when that chamomile tea just wasn't cutting it! You are all brilliant, thoughtful, kind, and giving, and I am so grateful for our little community.

To **Corey** and **Tasha Floyd** for helping me make the ferments for the photo shoot. I don't know how I thought I could get that work done without you. I could not have, and it would have been disastrous.

To my parents, **Nancy** and **Walt Feifer**, thank you for raising me to be independent and to pursue my own path, even if it has sometimes meant that I stressed you out by abandoning lucrative, corporate gigs in favor of the unknown.

To **Jake O'Brien**, my beloved, your support, kindness, hand-holding, love, understanding, and dishwashing abilities are unparalleled. There are so many things in my life I could not and cannot do without you. This was just one of those. Thank you for being by my side in all things.

And finally, to the **Phickle readers**, without you, I would never have continued pursuing this passion, teaching classes, and writing about fermentation. These things make me happy and fulfilled, and I'm eternally grateful to you for reading and fermenting along with me.

About the Author

Amanda Feifer writes about food fermentation of all kinds on her blog, phickle.com. When she's not concocting crazy vats of bubbly things in the kitchen or ranting against the use of antibacterial soaps, she's doing what she loves most: teaching people to make their own fermented foods, whether it's kimchi, koji, kefir, or kombucha. She lives in South Philly with her husband, Jake, and their rambunctious pit bull pup, Laika.